OUT
OF THE
FORTIES

By Nicholas Lemann

A FIRESIDE BOOK
Published by Simon & Schuster, Inc.
NEW YORK

All photographs in this volume are from the Standard Oil Collection, Photographic Archives, University of Louisville.

Portions of this book previously appeared in *Texas Monthly* and *The Atlantic*.

First Fireside Edition, 1985

Published by Simon & Schuster, Inc.
Simon & Schuster Building
Rockefeller Center
1230 Avenue of the Americas
New York, New York 10020

FIRESIDE and colophon are registered trademarks of Simon & Schuster, Inc.

Manufactured in the United States of America

10 9 8 7 6 5 4 3 2 1 Pbk.

Library of Congress Cataloging in Publication Data

Lemann, Nicholas.
    Out of the forties.

    "A Fireside book."
    1. United States—Social life and customs—1918-1945.
2. United States—Social life and customs—1945-1970.
3. United States—Description and travel—1940-1960.
4. Texas—Social life and customs.   5. Texas—Description
and travel.   I. Title.
E169.L54   1985   976.4'063   85-2356
ISBN 0-671-55419-0 Pbk.

Frontispiece: Street scene, Cushing, Oklahoma, 1946.

Photograph on pages 12 and 13: The garage of a house in Elk Basin, Wyoming, 1944; by Edwin Rosskam.

For D. B.

Contents

Acknowledgments

I owe the most thanks to Michael Lesy of Atlanta, who told me about the Standard Oil Collection and suggested that I might be interested in looking at it, and who, more important, showed me how to think about documentary photography as a starting point for historical inquiry. At the University of Louisville Photographic Archives, where the Standard Oil photographs reside, James C. Anderson and David Horvath were ceaselessly helpful and patient. So was William Carner, the printer of the pictures in this book, who deserves much of the credit for its coming into being. Thirty-five years after bringing the Standard Oil project to life, the photographers Esther Bubley and Russell Lee, and Sally Forbes, who was Roy Stryker's assistant, gave me their time and encouragement in generous measure. Princetta Johnson of Exxon and Marni Sandweiss of the Amon Carter Museum in Fort Worth were also of great help with the photographs.

Three of my former bosses who are also gifted teachers—William Greider, Richard Harwood, and Charles Peters—played large roles in getting me started on this book and in shaping my understanding of the forties. My present boss, Gregory Curtis, helped conceive and then edited the first part of my research, and was generous in giving me time to complete it. My editor at Texas Monthly Press, Daniel Okrent, was unerringly right in his extensive guidance throughout this project, and my agent, Amanda Urban, was equally astute in giving me guidance of a different sort. James Fallows read and made extensive and valuable suggestions on an early draft, and William Whitworth of *The Atlantic* helped me greatly with the first chapter.

The many people who were the subjects of my reporting provided the heart of this book, and it would be impossible to thank them enough. Like everyone else named here, they lent only worth to this project; its flaws are mine alone.

OUT OF THE FORTIES

1

THE PROJECT
A Picture of America

One Sunday evening during World War I, an infantry private at Camp Dix, New Jersey, wrote a long letter to his sister back home in Montrose, Colorado, describing his trip across the country in a troop train. The private's name was Roy Stryker, and he wrote on Army-Navy YMCA stationery, patriotically obeying an injunction printed at the bottom of each sheet to use both sides of the paper.

"We have had a very fine trip," he wrote. "We left Cody at 2:00 PM last Tuesday and arrived here last night (Saturday) or rather this morning about 3:00 AM. We came across N.M., Texas (the Panhandle), Okla., Kansas, Mo., Iowa, Illinois, Indiana, Ohio, Pennsylvania. We stopped for a short time in Kansas City, Chicago, Fort Wayne, Ind., Pittsburgh, Altoona, Pa., Harrisburg, and we came through Philadelphia some time during the night. It was a most interesting trip for a westerner, one who has been raised in the west and knows no other place."

He went on with the details at some length, and it is possible, reading the letter today, to discern in the young private the presence of a par-

Sol Libsohn

ticular eye. He seems to have formed in his mind an overall picture of America, coupled with an instinct for the specific visual cues that could best express what he felt. He was patriotic and sentimental, but also practical. He was drawn to simple, strong images of the country, but these could just as easily be industrial images as pastoral ones. The conflict between agriculture and technology seems not to have occurred to him, judging from the letter.

"Eastern Kansas held my attention," he wrote. "Rolling country, straw stacks, strips of trees fringing the creeks, cornfields, and occasionally the spire of the little country church with its cluster of white red-roofed houses about it. The whole country basked in the mellow sunshine and I know that these peaceful scenes made more than one of the boys quiet and thoughtful." It is hard to imagine a more deeply rural sensibility. But later in the trip, in Illinois, he seems just as stirred by the strength and clamor of machinery: "Our train stopped in the yards at Joliet across the river from the American Steel Wire Mills and such an ovation as we received and believe me it was appreciated from the shrill little toot of the steam shovel to the deep siren of the main plant. Screaming urchins with flags poured from the rows of smoke dimmed houses quickly recognizing the car loads of 'Khaki.' "

Full of brave resolve, he ended: "I would have liked to dropped in home today and enjoyed a Sunday at home. But a man can't allow his mind to stray when he is in the Army—there is one thing for all of us and that is over there."

Having gone, and come home, Roy Stryker enrolled at Columbia University, became an economics instructor there, and, eventually, arrived at the odd position that allowed him to supervise the taking of the

A sign in the doorway of an apartment house, New York City, 1946.

Two sailors on Walnut Street in Harrisburg, Pennsylvania, 1945.

Page 14: O. C. Green, a farmer, and his family outside a service station in Brown Summit, North Carolina. His son-in-law, in uniform, is home on furlough to help with planting the tobacco and harvesting the grain, 1944.

17

Edwin Rosskam

Monument commemorating the point farthest north reached by the Lewis and Clark expedition, between Browning and Cut Bank, Montana, 1944.

A ground crewman refueling a commercial airliner, Pittsburgh, Pennsylvania, 1948.

pictures on these pages. They come from a vast and ambitious photographic portrait of the country during and just after World War II, assigned and edited by Stryker in a way that brought out what he had seen and felt as a young man riding on a train to World War I.

As an instructor at Columbia in the 1920s, Stryker became an assistant to and protégé of Rexford Guy Tugwell, the New Deal brain truster. Stryker had begun to rely heavily on the use of photographs in his classes to give flesh and form to abstract economic principles,

Todd Webb

and when Franklin Roosevelt called Tugwell down to Washington to become assistant secretary of agriculture, Tugwell brought Stryker along, placed him in a division of the Agriculture Department called the Resettlement Administration (soon to be renamed the Farm Security Administration), and charged him with producing photographic evidence of the rural poverty of the Depression.

Stryker hired a group of young, social-conscienced photographers and sent them out on the road—among others, Walker Evans, Dorothea Lange, Russell Lee, Ben Shahn, Arthur Rothstein, and Carl Mydans—and they came back with a huge and sober body of work. The project was successful on three levels. First, the pictures were effective propaganda for the New Deal. Second, they provided the sustaining image of the Depression that most Americans hold in their minds even now. Pictures such as Lange's of a Dust Bowl mother and Evans's of bleached wooden small-town buildings rise above, say, Henry Fonda playing Tom Joad, or FDR speaking into a radio microphone, as the truest pictorial expression of those times. Finally, the FSA photographs have come to be regarded as works of art, and as such are the subject of several books, and (this would have horrified Stryker) are sold to the affluent and stylish by art galleries.

In 1943, Stryker left the government to work for Standard Oil of New Jersey (now called Exxon), which at that time was even less well loved than usual, having just been dragged through Senate hearings in which it was accused of war collaboration with I. G. Farben, the German chemical company. His job at Standard Oil was similar to what it had been at the FSA: to hire photographers to document the activities of Standard Oil in a way that would help create an influential and

A road in the Texas Panhandle, 1950.

Charles Rotkin

Passengers on a bus at the Greyhound Terminal in New York City, 1947.

John Vachon

Boys swimming off the 125th Street docks in New York City, 1947.

The Delta Queen, a Mississippi riverboat, heading north in the early evening, 1948.

benign image for the company among both the general public and its employees.

Naturally, there was some question whether Stryker, whose father had been a fervid Populist in Colorado, had forsaken his principles, but people who knew him say that by that time photographic documentation was a higher principle for him than New Deal politics. Standard Oil offered him the chance to mount a project much grander than the one he had run at the FSA. He could cover the world. He stayed at Standard Oil until 1950, when the project had begun to be scaled down because the company's polling showed that its image was improving only slightly. The project limped along under Stryker's successors until the middle fifties. Stryker moved to Pittsburgh to teach and to assemble photographs at the University of Pittsburgh and for several private employers. He died in 1975, at the age of eighty-two.

The Standard Oil of New Jersey Collection now resides in the University of Louisville's Photographic Archives, and contains 85,000 photographs, from which the selection in this book has been drawn. The collection stands as perhaps the best portrayal of the middle and late 1940s in any medium. The photographs show, first of all, the global operations of the world's largest company, with special emphasis on industrial plants. In fulfilling just that one purpose, they depict the loneliest reaches of the Rocky Mountains, placid towns in the South and Midwest, Rockefeller Center in New York City, and many examples of what was then high technology. There are pictures of Americans working in colonial splendor in Saudi Arabia, Venezuela, and other oil-producing countries that precisely convey the emotional background of OPEC's economic policies. And then there are photographs whose relation to Standard

Edwin Rosskam

Thomas Jefferson Robinson, the self-proclaimed "cat-skinner from Elk Basin," and his daughter Sally Jane sing a cowboy song at an amateur night, Powell, Wyoming, 1944.

Jars at a church harvest festival, Newark Valley, New York, 1945.

Oil is tangential in the extreme: street scenes of Paris and Rome and New York and Cushing, Oklahoma; riverboats on the Ohio and the Mississippi; New England fishermen, Texas cowboys, Southern plantation workers, Midwestern farmers, people in their living rooms, in the town café, and at their work. The only obvious bias in the collection is one toward photographs of people at and below the middle of the economic spectrum.

The photographers who took the pictures—a long list that includes Esther Bubley, Russell Lee, Harold Corsini, Edwin and Louise Rosskam, Gordon Parks, Todd Webb, John Vachon, John Collier, Jr., Berenice Abbott, Charlotte Brooks, and Elliott Erwitt—all worked for Stryker as free-lancers, and most of their assignments had some connection to a Standard Oil in-house publication. But there was flexibility. A story for the Standard magazine, *The Lamp*, could be about *users* of the company's products (that is, anybody) or the environs of a company plant, and, in addition, Stryker sent photographers returning from the road to shoot a roll or two at the New York docks, a favorite subject of his. Photographs from the project were made available to textbook publishers and to commercial magazines whose interests were far broader than the company's; once, a man writing about cloud formations asked Standard Oil for help with illustrations and was quickly provided with everything he needed from the incidental work of the Stryker project.

Quite often photographs convey to people looking at them years later a message that is different from what was intended at the time, but the Standard Oil pictures remain interesting for exactly the reasons that, as far as can be determined, they interested Stryker in the first place. They show a nation resolutely going about its

Charlotte Brooks

business, living mostly in a broad area between want and luxury, its roots still in the soil and the hamlet but by now enormously mighty as well. "Stryker was interested in the little details of American life," says Sally Forbes, who was his assistant during the best years of the Standard Oil project and now runs a small theater in Brooklyn. "He had white, flowing, curly hair and talked a mile a minute and was very vital and rigorous. He talked *so* fast. He always tried to tell the photographers what to do. He was a harsh critic. He was rigid. He hardly approved of anything, but he loved America. He loved it passionately, like an immigrant. As far as a born American who loved his country, I've never found anybody so profoundly devoted."

Looking at the pictures in the Standard Oil collection today, it is impossible to escape the feeling that a lesson must be contained in them. The moment they capture most vividly, immediately after World War II, is still easily within our collective memory, and it stands out as a watershed, the end of a long bad time and the beginning of a time of great confidence, prosperity, and change. The social and economic revolutions of the period make a familiar litany—the advent of affluence, the baby boom, the suburbs; the end of the war; the onward march of science; the rise to dominance of large organizations—but that doesn't make them any less significant. In 1946, the median family income in America ($21,000 today) was under $2,800, only 8,000 households had television sets, and 12.5 percent of people of college age went to college. ENIAC, the first high-speed digital computer (a vast, room-filling contraption), went into operation at the University of Pennsylvania. Commercial airlines flew 12 million passengers a year, compared to 300 million today. Nearly a fifth

Esther Bubley

The United Nations Building, New York City, 1951.

Fulton Fish Market, New York City, 1946.

27

Gordon Parks

Commuters on the ferry between Staten Island and Manhattan, 1946.

Schoolchildren from the mountains arriving in Asheville, North Carolina, to hear a concert, 1952.

of the population still lived on farms. The national consumer debt was less than a fortieth of what it is today. The ordinary life of Americans was just at the edge of a complete transformation.

One can certainly see all of this in the pictures: the kitchens barren of appliances, the kids without shoes. But there is an emotional richness to the pictures that is greater than a simple document of economic and social change would produce. They exert a complicated pull on us: they at once tap a reservoir of deep feelings about their time and create a curiosity about whether these feelings are consistent with the real life the pictures show so plainly.

Most Americans who were alive then, and especially those who are members of the opinion-making class, tend to regard the late forties as a peak moment in American history, a time of greater national power and nobility of purpose than now, and a time that, in the realm of everyday life, was better for being simpler. This view has been passed on to the generation that wasn't alive then, through books and movies, through millions of conversations at the dinner table, through bosses' reminiscences to young employees. It is possible when seeing these pictures to be convinced that the forties were the good old days. Look at the soldier returned to his home town to help with the harvest, or the family spending an evening in repose in the living room. There seems to have been a glue holding people together, making large national accomplishments possible.

On the other hand, look at the faces. They are faces you don't see often anymore, the urban ones immigrant-beefy, the rural ones sharecropper-worn. Even their moments of pleasure and repose seem to have come at a higher price than we are used to paying today. So a

Sol Libsohn

Truckers at the Eagle Grill, Akron, Ohio, 1945.

Waitress at a drive-in restaurant, Kemah, Texas, 1945.

second possible reaction to the pictures is to wonder whether the passing of that time deserves to be the occasion for lament that it generally is today.

Wondering which response was the right one, and wanting in any case to establish a closer and more satisfactory connection with the pictures and so between their time and our time, I began to retrace the steps of the photographers who took them. Thirty-five years later, I followed Esther Bubley (who was not yet twenty-five when she took most of the photographs and had just worked up to full photographer's status from an assistant's job in Stryker's lab at the FSA) to Tomball and Andrews, Texas, and to Linden, New Jersey. I followed Russell Lee (a former painter who had hung up his brushes and taken up photography, and had also worked on the FSA project) to the border agricultural area at the southern tip of Texas. I followed the husband-and-wife team of Edwin and Louise Rosskam to Baton Rouge, Louisiana, one of the stops on their long journey for the Standard Oil project down the Ohio and Mississippi rivers.

Some of these places were the remotest outposts of American life when the pictures were taken, oil-drilling towns in the middle of nowhere, and some of them are still remote today. Nonetheless, as I began to track down the people in the pictures—cowboys and engineers and oilmen—I found that their lives had changed dramatically in almost every case. The pictures are skewed somewhat toward the oil-producing areas of the country, which have changed faster than other places, but even outside oil country the people in the pictures, or their children, were far more prosperous than they had been thirty-five years before. Many had gone to college, or had sent their children. Quite often they thought, as a general proposition, that American

Sol Libsohn

life had gone downhill since those days, but their own lives had always gotten better.

As they told the stories of their lives, something besides simple material betterment emerged strongly— the phenomenon popularly decried as the breakdown of authority. Like the nation's newspaper columnists and politicians, the people in the pictures often complained that institutions are no longer accorded respect; that people are impatient and self-indulgent these days; that figures of authority—presidents, professors, clergymen, and the like—have lost much of their sway. But with much more immediacy, the breakdown of authority meant changes in the way power was exerted over the people themselves, and there is hardly anything that matters more than that.

Rather than diminishing, which it never really does, authority had taken different forms for the people in the pictures. They had generally moved in a direction the great sociologist Max Weber described seventy-five years ago, from life under traditional forms of authority to life under rational ones. In the forties, they had lived under the dominion of the standards of a town, or of an all-powerful boss, or of a parent, or of their local church. In the intervening years the power of these people and institutions had severely declined, and in their place large national organizations, operating strictly according to elaborate rules, had become more important. The perception that this had happened, when books like *The Organization Man* brought it to the fore, hit people hard because it represented such an immense shift in the world in which they had grown up. Instead of the town, there was a suburb whose merchants, architects, and employers were all huge national concerns. Instead of the boss, there was a corporation, or a federally funded university. What wasn't fully

Construction of the Esso Building in Rockefeller Center, New York City, 1946.

Stanley Rose, the manager of the Cleveland and Akron division of Anchor Motor Freight, a trucking company, 1945.

Gita Lenz

Times Square, New York City, 1952.

*Sorting racks for rural free delivery, at the
Winchester, Virginia, post office, 1947.*

perceived at the time was that these big institutions functioned less according to personal whim and more according to broad principles, and so meant more personal freedom, not less; they meant the freedom that comes from not being under the rule of any one person any longer.

One of the stories in this book is about a cowboy who was cuckolded by the rancher he worked for, but didn't dare leave his job. Another is about a murder case in Louisiana that might have become a civil rights case, but didn't, because in 1947 in rural Louisiana the people in charge didn't want it to be. Another is about a farm worker who had spent forty years working for a kindly, gift-bestowing boss, but who nonetheless was pushing his children to find jobs with the telephone company or the government, because he felt it wasn't good to be under one man for so long. All these stories concern people who were personally subjugated in ways they now feel would be impossible today. They stand as proof that the changes after the end of World War II released many people from some kind of trap, and so were a redemption of their dreams.

I don't present these people's existence as evidence that nostalgia for the forties is misplaced. Such things are impossible to prove or disprove, and anyway, the two seemingly opposing views of the meaning of these pictures are actually consistent with each other. What we sentimentally think of as changes for the worse since the forties and what the people I talked to experienced as changes for the better are in fact exactly the same changes. Simply put, as Americans have grown materially better off and personally freer, the old bonds of family and community have grown weaker, and from that has sprung an infinity of consequences that have touched us all.

2

LINDEN, NEW JERSEY
Industry

The device on the opposite page is called a fluid catalytic cracker; its function is to break up molecules of petroleum in order to extract from them as much gasoline as possible. It is a little-known invention that has become essential to the world, and it was first made during World War II on the grounds of the Standard Oil Company of New Jersey's Bayway Refinery in Linden, New Jersey. In the same place, at roughly the same time, were invented ultra-high-octane aviation fuel; synthetic butyl rubber; and a very popular insecticide of the period, sold commercially under the name Flit. It was a small flowering of the most practical kind of engineering, spurred on by the urgency of the war effort.

The Bayway Refinery was established in 1909 by the still undivided Standard Oil trust on a large tract of land just south of Elizabeth, New Jersey, on the narrow neck of water that separates the Jersey shore from Staten Island. It was for many years the world's largest oil refinery, a huge concentration of machinery and research laboratories, and in the forties it contained the sheer industrial muscle, the capacity for constant

Harold Corsini

innovation, and the sense of community that had carried the United States successfully through the war and into the period of enormous prosperity that followed, and then, somehow, seemed to disappear.

The crew-cut young man with rolled-up shirt sleeves in the picture on this page, William O. Taff, was the head of the team of engineers at Standard Oil Development Company in Bayway that developed the first catalytic cracker. In an earlier age he might have become a self-employed inventor, but he grew up at a time when the locus of technological innovation was shifting decisively from the individual to the large organization. In the early 1920s, when Taff was a baby, nearly three times as many patents on inventions were issued to individuals as to corporations; by 1980, when he retired, that figure had been neatly reversed: nearly three times as many patents went to corporations as to individuals.

Will Taff had grown up in Bowling Green, Kentucky, studied chemical engineering at the University of Illinois, and gone to work for Standard Oil right after graduation in 1939. In 1941, at the age of 23, he was put in charge of a team assigned to develop a working prototype that would put to practical use everything that was then known about catalytic cracking. They did what engineers do: found the optimum conditions and production values, brought down the cost, refined endlessly. When they were done, fluid catalytic cracking was instantly adopted as part of the process of refining oil, and the team turned to other problems in the endless work of technology.

Taff went on to become an executive with Standard, and he retired after 41 years with the company. I went see him at his house in Westfield, New Jersey, a pretty little suburban town west of Elizabeth. He didn't look much like his picture. His hair had lain down over

William O. Taff in the labs, Bayway Refinery, Linden, 1944.

Overalls hung on a clothesline to dry, Baytown Refinery, Baytown, Texas, 1946.

Page 36: Fluid catalytic cracker, Bayway Refinery, Linden, 1947.

Esther Bubley

Pete Schiessl at a meeting of the pinochle club, Bayway Community Center, Elizabeth, New Jersey, 1944.

Building a fluid catalytic cracker at Bayway Refinery, Linden, 1949.

the years and now it was white, and while he was healthy, he was no longer husky. He was quiet and direct. He had a beautifully tended backyard. What complaints he had about the world today were mild. They had to do with industry and its movement away from the center of life. After the war, the development labs at Bayway had been moved across U.S. Highway 1 into a group of low-slung buildings that look like the campus of a small college, and there they have stayed, dissociated from the refinery. The engineers, he said, didn't have their hands on the real machinery anymore.

In 1948, a large new cat cracker was built at Bayway, and during the construction it was discovered that a huge hemispherical piece of metal intended to be the top of a vat needed to be trimmed by three-quarters of an inch. It was sent back to the machine shop, where a machinist named Pete Schiessl, doing the work, slipped and caught a red-hot piece of steel in his eye. Company doctors took out the steel and came close to taking out the eye too, but then decided to wait, and Schiessl's eye healed to the point that he got most of his sight back. He considered himself lucky and was grateful to the company.

He is the sober-looking man dressed in a heavy, neat suit in the picture on this page. He's playing pinochle on a Tuesday evening at the Bayway Community Center in Elizabeth, an institution in large part responsible for his warm feelings toward Standard Oil and one that could not—indeed, does not—exist today. It began in 1919 when Abby Aldrich Rockefeller, the wife of John D. Rockefeller, Jr., had a sturdy two-story brick cottage built on Bayway Avenue as an example of the kind of house in which she felt the workers of the Rockefellers' company should live. The workers, im-

migrants or the children of immigrants from Poland, Italy, and Czechoslovakia, lived in wood-frame houses that were not quite up to Mrs. Rockefeller's standards but weren't bad either, and her cottage grew over the years into a complex that covered a whole city block. It had a nursery, a basketball court, an infirmary, a bowling alley, a kitchen, and several spacious meeting rooms. From the mid-thirties to the mid-sixties, it was run by a stern, kind-hearted woman named Ethel Mathiasen, the wife of a local businessman, known to everyone as Mrs. M. Her picture is on this page.

"I was in deep concern," Mrs. Mathiasen said when I showed her the picture. She is small, formal, even a little regal, and lives in a big white Colonial-style house. "And I know what the concern was. One of my teenagers was having a hard time and he'd been put out of school for fighting and he'd gone to court. I spent every Tuesday evening at juvenile court for my boys. I went back the next day and spoke with the judge, and there seemed to be little hope that he wouldn't be sent away. And I was dejected. The boy was a fighter. He fought brutally. But the judge turned it back to me: I was the boy's parole officer for six months. And one day I found out he'd been in another fight across the street from the center. I said, 'How could you have done this to me?' He said, 'You have it all wrong, Mrs. M. I have so much respect for you that I dragged him off your property before I beat him.' I had to laugh. There was a spark there that you had to like."

In the present, she laughed again, and began telling me stories about the center—the personal concern and frequent visits of Mrs. Rockefeller, her insistence that everyone from the neighborhood, not just Standard employees, be allowed to use the center, the quality of the medical care, the trusting quality of the small

Ethel Mathiasen in her office at the Bayway Community Center, Elizabeth, New Jersey, 1953.

Teenagers dancing at the Bayway Community Center, Elizabeth, New Jersey, 1953.

Esther Bubley

At the baby clinic of the Bayway Community Center, Elizabeth, New Jersey, 1944.

children, the spunk of the teenage girls, the loyalty of the annuitants, the gaiety of the mothers on their rare nights off. She told me the story of the center's getting the first television in the neighborhood and of the teenagers sitting in rows in front of it in the evenings, spellbound—you can see the scene in the picture on page 45. She told me about the classes in Americanization she conducted in the old days, teaching English-language literacy and U.S. history to the workers and their wives. She told me how she had befriended the first black family to move into the neighborhood after the war, the Watkinses, enrolled their daughter Devorah in the nursery school, and eventually made Eunice Watkins director of the baby clinic.

In 1963 the company moved the headquarters for its operations to Houston, and Mrs. Mathiasen began to feel that the center's days were numbered. Her superiors began to tell her that one refinery couldn't be singled out for special treatment, and the fees charged at the center began to go up. She retired in 1966, and two years later the company sold the center to the local United Way chapter. The United Way soon moved to another building, and for a time the local Catholic Charities office occupied space there; but now the center is in bad disrepair, and its doors are shut with heavy padlocked chains, and there is a For Sale sign out front.

"The people working for Standard had gone through a training," said Eunice Watkins, who still lives in Linden and whose picture is on page 46, by way of explaining why the center had been sold. "But after a while they were beginning to evolve to self-sufficiency. So the policy became to make people pay for what they were getting. They began to want to know, how many dollars per child per day? I know; I used to meet with those men."

Boys watching an early television set at the Bayway Community Center, Elizabeth, New Jersey, 1948.

Esther Bubley

Eunice Watkins with children in the nursery school, Bayway Community Center, Elizabeth, New Jersey, 1953.

Nursery school students at the Bayway Community Center, Elizabeth, New Jersey, 1944.

"In the beginning it was in the interest of the company to acculturate the workers," said her daughter Devorah, who now lives in New York and learned her business terminology at the Harvard Business School. "Then they get acculturated, and you get rational managers, and the relationship between the company and the workers is not so strong."

With great fervor, Eunice Watkins told me the story of how she had placed Devorah in the center. "We were our natural selves," she said. "We arrived, and we were as we always were. Those immigrants read us very well—what we wore, what we said. We had high visibility. And when I became director of the nursery, I had to walk a tightrope. I could not fail. I wrote memos in triplicate because people were waiting for me to make a mistake. And you know what? It made me hard but it made me damn good at what I do. I had earned it. I really earned it." She made it clear that she considered the days of the center better days than now, although plainly the center had been for her, as it was for the immigrants, a means of transition into a world where industrial paternalism seems quaint. Devorah, as a student at Radcliffe, roomed with Peggy Rockefeller, Abby's granddaughter.

But Mrs. Watkins' case rested solely on the notion of community, which was diminished. "It was a gradual thing," she said, half-watching Devorah's daughter play in her warm kitchen. "It just started eroding. It was just like something glued together falling apart."

Pete Schiessl, now 82, lives a couple of blocks from the old community center, in a house he moved into when it was built in 1925. He is active in the affairs of the company's annuitants, but he misses the same things Mrs. Watkins misses. He was not very eager to

Edwin Rosskam

A laboratory worker, Baytown Refinery, Baytown, Texas, 1944.

talk about them, but his son Donald, who sat by him when I came to visit, was.

"The refinery in this community was the place to work," Donald said. "They treated their employees very, very good. But then in fifty-seven, fifty-eight, they began to review the refinery and they decided they had too many people. So they laid off a number of hourly people and offered early retirement to foremen like my dad. That hurt. My father was hurt. The people of his day and age, when they worked for an employer, they were dedicated. They called at three a.m., they came down there. They worked. And then the company gave them early outs. They said, 'Okay, guys, that's it.' The guys just didn't think that was ever gonna happen. They were too good a company. My dad was bitter. He never had a retirement party. He just walked out that gate."

Pete Schiessl was uncomfortable with this talk, and he shifted in his lounge chair. "Now, thirty years, they give you a clock," he said, by way, I thought, of exculpating the company. "Then, what could you do?"

A worker at the control board of the hydroformer unit, Baytown Refinery, Baytown, Texas, 1950.

The man pointing his finger in the picture on page 50 is Oliver G. Lewis; the man next to him is Kenny Griffith; they're in the control booth of an ugly one-room concrete shell called a test stand. The concrete wall above the two men's heads in the picture was twenty inches thick, and covered with white sound-absorbing tiles and studded with heavy-duty lights. The glass in front of them was four panes thick. All that protection was against the terrific noise—132 decibels—emitted by the huge stripped-down aviation engine on which the man lifting equipment is working in the picture on page 53. The engine, mounted in the center of the test stand, would be fed with a particular kind of fuel and Oliver Lewis, behind the glass, would watch.

The purpose of the test stand was to serve as a laboratory for the development of extremely high-octane fuel for fighter and transport planes in the war. The higher the octane, the more efficiently a plane's engine could run, and so the less fuel it would need to carry. When wars were thought to be won or lost on logistics, these were vital matters. By early 1945, Oliver

Gordon Parks

Oliver Lewis and Kenny Griffith in the high-octane aviation fuel test stand, Linden, 1944.

The wife of a serviceman at work in the Baytown Refinery, Baytown, Texas, 1944.

Lewis and his crew had produced fuel with an octane rating of 165; before the war, 100-octane was the highest-rated fuel available. They developed a fuel that was, improbably enough, fire-retardant, so that a fighter plane that got a tracer bullet through its gas tank wouldn't explode. The engineers, the company, and the government had found a harmony with one another that, in other forms and in many places, would continue to thrive after the war was over and would work to diminish the quirky, personal side of organizational life that animated the Bayway Community Center, and, in fact, Oliver Lewis himself.

When I showed Oliver Lewis the pictures of the test stand, it obviously brought back pleasant memories for him. He left me in his sitting room and went off to find his scrapbooks, so that I could be given a guided tour of his life as an inventor. He lives in Mountainside, New Jersey, in a neat house with an American flag flying out front. When he had returned and spread before me a mass of old photographs, schematic drawings, the guest register from the aviation fuel test stand, and clippings from company publications and the local papers, he told me he had grown up in Indianapolis. His father was the superintendent of a Bethlehem Steel plant, and from early childhood he had been interested in machinery, especially automobile engines. He got a degree in mechanical engineering from Purdue in 1935, considered job offers from Chrysler and Standard Oil, and, figuring that the oil industry was more stable than the automotive industry, picked Standard.

He worked in Bayonne for a while and then moved to Bayway, and by the time the war began he was a lieutenant in the Army Reserves and expected to be called up. But the company got him a deferment to do his work on aviation fuels. In 1943, the test stand was built

to his specifications and he ran it until 1946, when he moved across the highway to the new research center. He developed new specifications for the distributors in automotive engines. He invented a machine called the mileage accumulation dynamometer, in which cars could take simulated road trips and be tested for fuel efficiency without ever venturing outside. He was widely quoted as saying that teenagers who listen to rock 'n' roll use 50 percent more fuel because they tap their feet on the accelerator pedal. He developed a machine to take the viscosity level of fluids. He developed a machine to splice inner tubes made of butyl rubber. "I've done everything under the sun," he said, by way of summing it up.

Now he was ready to tell me about his great invention. He showed me a drawing of a service station that looked futuristic, but in a way that said more about the fifties, when it was made, than about the future as it turned out. In particular, the gasoline pumps looked odd, full of dials and tubes, and this was because they contained an automatic oil changer. In the future as Lewis imagined it, you would fill up your gas tank and at the same time open your hood and stick a tube into your crankcase, which would automatically suck out all the engine oil and replace it with clean oil.

For the automatic oil changer to work, it was first necessary for the auto manufacturers to outfit the crankcases of cars with a small 34-cent part, so Lewis made a prototype out of clear plastic and took it to Detroit. General Motors and Ford said, as he remembers it, "if you can get your machine in the service stations, we'll have five men on it tonight." This was exciting news. He went back to Standard, convinced he was about to bring about a small but memorable step in the continual betterment of American life through technology. But

A workman in the high-octane aviation fuel test stand, Linden, 1944.

Workers painting a crude oil storage tank, Baytown Refinery, Baytown, Texas, 1946.

Edwin Rosskam

A deckhand on a barge in the Ohio River, 1945.

A foreman at the Structural Steel Company in New York City, 1946.

the company said no. The cost of the oil changers was $1500 apiece, and to re-equip every Standard service station would be too expensive. That was what they said, anyway. Lewis felt that the real reason the marketing people didn't like the idea was that the research people had come up with it. It was his great moment of disillusionment.

Nonetheless, he stayed with Standard. The day of the toolshed mechanical tinkerer who clears the path of industry had long passed, and the great consolation that organizational life could offer was that it went smoothly on. He developed a miniature jet engine in a glass tube, a specially outfitted car called a rolling laboratory, and an automatic coffee maker. He retired in 1974, but he still goes down to the office. I asked him how he thought life was different now from the old days of the test stand.

"It used to be . . ." he said, and thought for a minute, "it's like my father. He didn't even graduate from high school, and yet he was superintendent of a Bethlehem Steel unit. You went into a business and you got your hands dirty. Now they go skiing in Colorado. It's the fellas that've gotten their hands dirty that can tell you how the engine works."

He went on: "Damn it, I've had to correct them. A Ph.D., it's book learning. A Ph.D.'s fine in research, but to find out what goes on in the actual world . . ." He shook his head. "I don't know. The new math was the great fiasco of our times. You take away these kids' computers and they can't find their way home. My idea is that you don't have to keep your head crammed with ideas, you just need to know where to get them." He straightened up his old pictures and clippings a little and gave me a level look. "That's the way it is at the present time," he said crisply.

3

ELSA, TEXAS
Americanization

At the most extreme southern tip of the mainland United States, in the part of Texas where the Rio Grande meets the Gulf of Mexico, there is an area known, by wild misnomer, as the Valley. It is flat, arid, and hot; its largest city, Brownsville, is well known to followers of the weather reports as perennially one of the hottest places in the country. White men first gazed upon the Valley in 1519, when an expedition led by the Spanish explorer Alvarez de Pineda went ashore at the mouth of the Rio Grande and traded with an encampment of Indians. In the nineteenth century, there was a bustling commercial barge trade on the lower Rio Grande, and the Valley was a part of the disputed territory over which the Mexican War was fought. But it was mostly a remote part of the frontier, a place whose history is filled with fierce battles in which the victors' spoils were pathetically small.

The Valley's present condition has its roots in the first decades of this century, when a group of promoters and boosters figured out how to make more money out of it than anyone else had for 400 years. First they

Russell Lee

induced the Missouri-Pacific Railroad to build a line to Brownsville, which was completed in July 1904 and immediately extended fifty miles upriver to the town of McAllen. Then they formed a series of private irrigation companies that pumped water out of the river and into inland reservoirs and irrigation canals—and suddenly the Valley was suitable for year-round vegetable farming. Its silty desert soil was extremely fertile when irrigated; the climate was ideal for a winter growing season; and with the railroad, produce could be shipped out to market.

The promoters planted tall palm trees at regular intervals along the major roads and put forth the notion that the Valley was a glamorous tropical paradise. Then they brought down trainloads of freezing Midwesterners and convinced them to buy winter homes or retirement homes or lots in trailer parks, and in time the Valley became a mecca for the elderly. Meanwhile rough and ambitious men, also coming from the North, moved in and established themselves in the vegetable and citrus businesses. And these groups were both dwarfed by the constant stream of people who got across the river one way or another, fleeing hunger and political upheaval in Mexico, and looked for work in the vegetable fields.

There were, then, at least three cultural layers to life in the Valley: the plantation style of life that the rich growers tried to establish for themselves; the genteel, sleepy, middle-class life of the retirees and the middle-aged bourgeoisie; and the life of the immigrants, with their meager shacks that lacked electricity and running water. Immigration to the United States, according to the Census Bureau, peaked in 1910, but that is hard to believe from the vantage point of the Mexican border. The Valley and other places like it have become the

Russell Lee

The headquarters of the annual Citrus Fiesta, Mission, Texas, 1948.

Main Street decorated for the Citrus Fiesta, Mission, Texas, 1948.

Page 56: An aerial view of the lower Rio Grande, 1948.

Russell Lee

Truck farmers selling tomatoes in the Farmers' Market, Houston, Texas, 1947.

Crowd at the Citrus Fiesta, Mission, Texas, 1948.

Ellis Islands of the second half of the century.

It is possible to offer up the Valley as a metaphor for a particularly cynical view of the United States. Everything there is an illusion created by an almost desperate yearning for economic gain. It isn't really farmland, only a desert robbing a great river of its water. It isn't really a wonderful, lovely retirement spot, just a flat plain oddly punctuated by neat lines of palm-tree tops. As for the immigrants, if they came to America hoping to find equality and prosperity, what they got, for many years, was a dollar or two a day for picking vegetables. Of course, the same facts could be used to make the case for the Valley as an inspiring place where several varieties of the human spirit have triumphed over considerable adversity. Either way, it is an inconclusive exercise. The Valley isn't Athens or even Plymouth by any stretch of analogy, but the people who go there usually find something they want, and they get by.

Fred Henry Vahlsing came to the Valley in 1909, at the age of 19. He was the son of a German immigrant who had settled in Maspeth, Long Island, and died in an accident at a construction site. His mother established a vegetable farm in Maspeth, the produce from which her two boys would hawk from pushcarts in New York City. Fred Vahlsing, having read pulp literature about the Wild West, decided there was something beyond Maspeth. Mentally locating it in Texas, he booked passage on a steamer for Jacksonville, Florida, and then rode a coal car to Houston. There he worked as a movie projectionist for a time, until someone told him about the developments afoot in the Valley, and he took off south, intending to get into the vegetable business. He settled in Elsa, a dusty little village in the up-

Russell Lee

Children watching electric trains in a downtown store window in Harlingen, Texas, 1947.

per Valley, fifteen miles north of the Rio Grande and thirty miles in from the Gulf. He hung around, slept outside, and accumulated enough money here and there to begin acquiring land at $10 an acre. He started a farm. In 1917 he shipped a train carload of fresh produce to Newark, New Jersey, riding with the vegetables and shoveling snow into the car along the way to keep them fresh. They were still fresh when he arrived, and they fetched $3,182—the first Texas winter vegetables to be sold on the East Coast.

By the late 1940s, when Russell Lee took the pictures on these pages in and around the Vahlsing farms, Fred Vahlsing had built an empire. He was the biggest grower in the Valley, some said the biggest individual farmer in the country. He had everything from Elsa to Edinburg under cultivation, a span of eleven miles. He owned 27,000 acres of farmland in the Valley, as well as substantial farms in Maine, New Jersey, California, New York, and Virginia. He built an ice house and invented a machine to blow shaved ice into the railroad cars that carried his vegetables north. He introduced broccoli into popular use in this country, mostly as a specialty vegetable to be shipped to Little Italy in New York. Along the railroad tracks in Elsa, he built the world's largest packing shed, 5000 feet long and 60 feet wide, and he shipped out 100 carloads of vegetables a day. He was in all sorts of businesses in other places. He had an office in New York and several homes. He employed 11,000 people, chief among them his son and heir, Fred, Jr.

A couple of miles north of Edinburg, just off U.S. Highway 281, is the old plant of Vahlsing Ice and Cold Storage, a hulking, seedy presence that stands next to a rusty set of railroad tracks. Part of the plant is an ice factory, barely in use anymore, a huge, drafty place; and part is a cold storage room to which an ominous metal sliding door is the only entry. Just outside stands a beat-up trailer with a couple of desks inside that serves as the office, and it was there that I found Ezequiel Granado, the manager, whose picture is on page 65. He was thick in the middle without being fat. He had iron gray hair and a thin moustache. His friends from the old days had told me his nickname was Cheke, a Spanish diminutive, but the plastic nameplate on his desk identified him as Zeke.

He told me his parents had been born in Mexico and had come to America in the teens. His father's family decided to try life in Houston, but, worried about whether it would work, they left Zeke's father behind in the safer harbor of an uncle's house in the Valley. He quarreled with the uncle, and after he left he was somehow adopted by a Texas Ranger named Puckett, who raised him while also employing him as his houseboy. He met Zeke's mother in the Valley in the mid-1920s, married her, left the Pucketts, and moved to Baytown, Texas, a refinery town outside of Houston. It was there, on the Fourth of July, 1927, that Zeke was born. Later that year his parents decided they didn't like Baytown so they moved back to Elsa and his father got a job with Vahlsing. Neither of the Granados had formal schooling, both were illiterate, and neither spoke anything but Spanish. They had eleven children who lived three or four to a room in a house with no hot water and no bathroom. In the summers when the vegetable business was slack, the whole family would migrate to West Texas and pick cotton.

Zeke began working part-time for Vahlsing in 1939, when he was 12 years old, tying bunches of broccoli after school. At 14 he applied at the county court-

Part of the crowd at the Citrus Fiesta, Mission, Texas, 1948.

Russell Lee

house for a special permit that would allow him to be paid an hourly wage even though he was a minor. At 16, he quit school to begin working full-time because his family was having trouble getting by, and a few months later he was drafted into the Army. He came back to the Valley in early 1947. He pointed out to me with some ardor that the picture of him, taken in the spring of 1947, must have been posed, because by that time he was already keeping time cards, making out bills, and doing other work around the office. He was completely devoted to getting ahead. In 1950, he enrolled in a night vocational school under the G.I. Bill and in three years had gotten a diploma in business administration. He married in 1951 and left Vahlsing for a job with another produce company. But in 1954, he left that job to become a loading foreman at the Vahlsing ice house in Edinburg, and he has been there ever since.

The time after the war, he said, was when things began to change for the Mexicans in the Valley. In Elsa in the days of his youth, all the Anglos had lived south of the railroad tracks, and they had owned every business in town. Then the Mexicans started a couple of grocery stores and a pharmacy. A few Mexican families moved south of the tracks. The public elementary schools, which were institutions even more crucial in Elsa than elsewhere because they were where the Mexican kids learned to speak English, were integrated. The war had shown a larger world to the young men of the town—Zeke served in Germany—and given them a greater sense of being Americans. The G.I. Bill made higher education and therefore real economic advancement a possibility for them for the first time. New waves of immigrants were still coming across the river and finding their way to the fields and packing sheds, living in rented shacks or out in the fields, but the Mexi-

Russell Lee

Ezequiel Granado packing tomatoes in F. H. Vahlsing's big shed at Elsa, 1947.

Workers in the Vahlsing broccoli fields, Edcouch, Texas, 1948.

Russell Lee

A string bean picker and his daughter sacking peas, near Harlingen, Texas, 1947.

Irrigated cotton fields near Hidalgo, Texas, 1952.

cans born in the United States were beginning to come up in the world.

Zeke Granado was a foreman in the Vahlsing ice house until 1960. Then he became assistant manager and finally, in 1978, manager. In 1960 Fred Vahlsing, Jr., gave him a plot of land containing a broken-down old house, just across the street from the ice house, and Zeke rebuilt it into a red-brick suburban rambler, with a two-car garage and a den. The house is really indistinguishable from the house of a middle-class Anglo, except that it is next to an ice house rather than in a real neighborhood. The Granados have six children. Four are graduates of Pan American University, a ten-year-old school in Edinburg that is obviously the product of a time when federal education money flowed more freely than it does now. Of the remaining two children, one is a senior at Pan American and the other is a sophomore there. Only one of the children is married, and to an Anglo. A more on-the-money story of immigrants' progress would be difficult to imagine, as Zeke himself, despite his air of fierce uncomplicatedness, was well aware.

In the lobby of the Echo Motel in Edinburg, a tropically genteel product of the fifties that is the social gathering place of choice in the upper Valley, I met Fred Vahlsing, Jr. He pulled up in a big, worn blue Ford LTD convertible with his little girl, Annie, and her Mexican-American nurse. He was a tall, gangling man in his mid-fifties, wearing a big floppy straw hat and a rough pullover garment made of black cotton over white slacks. Where his right hand would have been, there was a hook.

He told me with great enthusiasm the story of his father, who had died of heart failure back in 1969. It

Russell Lee

Russell Lee

A worker with a load of oranges at the Valley Fruit Company, Pharr, Texas, 1948.

A load of radishes in the Vahlsing packing shed, Elsa, 1947.

turned out that 1947, when Russell Lee took these pictures, was for the Vahlsing business an apex from which there followed an inexorable decline. There had been a killing freeze in January 1949 and another, worse one in January 1951. Then frozen vegetables came along. "Dad always said fresh is the best," Vahlsing told me. "He said, 'They sell six ounces for thirty-nine cents. I sell a pound and a half for nineteen cents.' Back then frozen was just a foot on the grocery shelf. In the forties, there was really nothing *but* fresh. Boston used to take twenty cars of spinach a night!

"Now," he said, "it's convenience America. It's frozen. It's Burger King. It's McDonald's. People used to *cook* vegetables in this country." He made it clear that this was a sad comment on matters far beyond the vegetable business. I asked him what he was doing now. "I'm in real estate in a modest way down here," he said. What happened to the great Vahlsing farms? "Dad knew every nut and bolt in the place," he said. "I never did the farming. I wish he'd lived to be a hundred. When he died there was nobody who was a farmer. It all went away." He gave me a sad smile that made it clear there would be no further explanation. Obviously, the years had been in some way less kind to him than they had been to Zeke Granado, his lifelong employee.

Vahlsing went on his way, and I went downtown to the Hidalgo County courthouse and looked for lawsuits under the name Vahlsing. There were many of them. Like many rural county clerks, Hidalgo's wasn't a record-keeper of the first order. Quite a few of the cases were missing, and the records of those that weren't were rarely complete. But it was possible to piece together what had happened in rough outline.

During the time of the death of his father, every

conceivable kind of trouble had befallen Fred Vahlsing, Jr. He was divorced. He lost his right hand in a helicopter accident. Although he had been a good student himself—he is a member of Phi Beta Kappa, with engineering degrees from Tufts and Princeton—his two sons both dropped out of boarding schools. Those portions of the Vahlsing empire located in Maine came under attack from environmentalists for polluting a creek. Various critics of the 1972 presidential aspirations of Senator Edmund Muskie became interested in the Muskie-Vahlsing relationship, particularly as it touched on the Vahlsing farms in Maine and Muskie's sponsorship of agricultural legislation. Vahlsing's telephone was tapped by Donald Segretti, of the Nixon plumbers. These were his minor problems.

In 1970, he became financially involved in an extremely complex fashion with Dr. Armand Hammer, the octogenarian who runs Occidental Petroleum. Dr. Hammer had known the senior Vahlsing as a fellow gentleman cattle rancher in New Jersey, and after the old man's death, Fred, Jr., later testified, Hammer took him aside and sketched out a vision of their future as business partners: "He said that someday I would be president of Occidental Petroleum Corporation and that we would be—that we would do great things together." Occidental took effective control of certain of the Vahlsing operations. On November 20, 1970, Dr. Hammer wrote Vahlsing a personal check for one million dollars, which Vahlsing testified was a business loan. Vahlsing didn't pay back the loan, and Hammer foreclosed on the Vahlsing lands that were the collateral. In the summer of 1972 Hammer told Vahlsing he was "severing the umbilical cord" and their odd relationship was over.

The Vahlsing companies, a staggeringly long list (Xonu Corporation, Valco, Texas Plastics, Trenton

Russell Lee

A woman wrapping a head of cauliflower on F. H. Vahlsing's Panchita Ranch, near Edcouch, Texas, 1948.

A truckload of onions on the way to market, Louisiana, 1947.

John Vachon

Women packing lima beans into boxes for freezing, at Seabrook Farms, near Bridgeton, New Jersey, 1947.

Women packing broccoli in the Vahlsing shed, Elsa, 1947.

Robinsville Airport, Maine Sugar Industries, Margarita Oil, Lorelei Company, Agro Resources, Inc., to name just a few), began to go under. Vahlsing Christina Corporation, the old man's holding company, forfeited its charter in 1974, owing millions in back taxes. Vahlsing, Inc., a frozen foods subsidiary, went bankrupt. In the summer of 1981, Texas Plastics went bankrupt, and on March 29, 1982, Fred Henry Vahlsing, Jr., filed for personal bankruptcy. He claimed assets of $3,212.81 and obligations of $5.6 million to creditors and $990,000 to the Internal Revenue Service. Surely, it was mostly his fault, but it was possible to think of him as having fallen victim to the modern world, with its many complications, rules, and regulations (he told me his father barely kept any books at all in his prime), and its insufficient appreciation of fresh vegetables.

One of Zeke Granado's children works as an accountant in the comptroller's office at Pan American University. Another is assistant director of the computer center at Pan American. Two more teach school in the Valley. The one who is about to graduate from college is an accounting major. "He'll probably apply with Southwestern Bell, Exxon—the *big* companies," Zeke told me proudly. "They're looking out for what we didn't look out for in the forties: benefits, retirement plans, et cetera." He hastened to add that he had also admonished them to work hard, be honest, and pay attention to older people, but it was plain that his real message to them was to seek out their fortunes in big, secure bureaucracies.

This was at odds with Zeke's stated view of the modern world, which was grumbling disapproval. He said there were too many unions and too much government red tape, making it hard to do business anymore.

Russell Lee

Russell Lee

He said he hated it when people applying for jobs with him asked right off the bat whether there would be insurance for their families. Like his father before him, he had spent virtually all his life in the employ of the Vahlsings, so his relationship with authority has been one of patronage. His pay was never high, and he had never worked under a retirement plan; on the other hand, he had received impulsive personal gifts (like his house) that in a sense reinforced his subordination but that he wouldn't have gotten elsewhere. In return he was adamantly loyal to Fred Vahlsing, Jr. He feigned unfamiliarity with Vahlsing's business reverses. If he knew that Vahlsing had lost the ice house in bankruptcy and now supposedly managed it (though Zeke did that, really) for one of his former creditors, he didn't let on. It was very clear in his own mind that he was still working for Mr. Vahlsing.

A large citrus packing house in Pharr, Texas, 1948.

It seemed to me that his children's lives represented a truer expression of his feelings than what he said; my guess was that he took a dimmer view of the two-generation transaction between the Granado family and the Vahlsing family than he preferred to admit. He told me that after the last child finished college he planned to leave and start his own business. The children themselves would have an entirely different relationship to authority than his—they would be employed in organizations where power resides in rules more than in individual people. But if this was what Zeke wanted, and if it was to him the last great step his family needed to take, there was no reason to expect him to say so.

In Elsa there is a long bare patch of grass where the old Vahlsing packing shed used to be, right next to the railroad tracks that divide the town north and south. The shed closed down in 1950 and was demolished a

A crew of day farm laborers waits to be driven to the next job, Harlingen, Texas, 1945.

Russell Lee

Unloading cabbages from the fields at the Vahlsing packing shed, Elsa, 1947.

Joaquin Guerrero washing a load of beets in the Vahlsing packing shed, Elsa, 1947.

few years later. Some of the vast vegetable fields are still there, but most of them have been converted to citrus groves. Elsa does not present itself as a town undergoing rapid change. There isn't much there that is new, quite a few of the streets are still unpaved, and chickens and goats in front yards are a common sight. Even though the packing shed is long gone, quite a few of the people who used to work in it are still in Elsa. One is Luis Joaquin Guerrero, the man spraying a truckload of beets in the picture on page 77.

The Guerrero home is of single-wall wood, with a beautiful little flower garden in front. I wasn't invited past the front room, but there appeared to be two rooms in all, a living room and a bedroom-kitchen. I didn't see an indoor bathroom. The front room was decorated, as so many poor people's front rooms are today, mainly with graduation pictures; Catholic hagiography was a subsidiary theme. At the center of the room was a color television set on which a Spanish-language soap opera about the romantic difficulties of sophisticated young city people was playing. In the immigrant culture of the Valley, times do change somewhat, but by far the most important determinant of how someone lives is how far removed generationally he is from the crossing of the Mexican border. Thus the Guerreros, with a few accoutrements of the modern world they had gathered around them, corresponded to Zeke Granado's parents.

Joaquin Guerrero speaks no English and his wife, Dolores, knows only a few words, so the seventh of their nine children, Idolina, a 27-year-old teacher's aide, translated for me. She said her father was born in 1910 in the town of San Felipe in the Mexican state of Guanajuato. In 1916 his parents, fleeing the Mexican Revolution and lacking enough to eat, sneaked across the border at Laredo, Texas. Joaquin grew up working on

Russell Lee

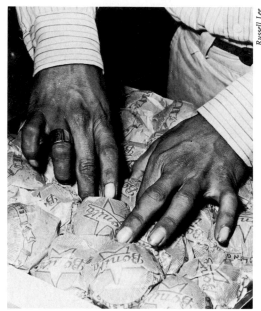

Russell Lee

The hands of Joaquin Guerrero, Elsa, 1947.

farms, and in 1942 he came to Elsa and convinced Victor Zavala, the foreman of the packing shed, to give him a job. He packed ice, packed vegetables, counted bushels, washed vegetables. In 1954 he left and began taking his family around the country to work the vegetable harvests—Texas, Florida, Michigan; tomatoes, cherries, cucumbers, eggplants. In 1968 he contracted tuberculosis and moved everyone back to Elsa, where he does odd jobs around town. Of the nine children, eight are married, four have finished high school, and only one works in the vegetable fields. "Me, I'm going to college right now," Idolina said. "My mother emphasized education. My daddy was always for the field, to make money. But now he realizes that you have to have an education to get anywhere. That's what he tells me most of the time. Finish college."

I noticed that Joaquin was wearing a simple metal ring with two or three crosswise grooves—the very ring on the hand of the tomato-packer on this page. He looked at the picture, nodded, and took off the ring. Underneath was a band of light skin. He told Idolina he had made the ring long ago out of a piece of pipe. Then he motioned to her and delivered a brief, animated speech, and sank back into his battered easy chair, satisfied. A pretty girl was sobbing on the television screen. "He says at that time he was worried because of the Great Depression and he was always worried that there may not be work," said Idolina. "Now, he feels he can really support his family without having to worry about there being work. He says he's proud of America and grateful because he found food and shelter for his sons and daughters which he probably wouldn't have got in Mexico. He's proud of that. And he's grateful." He motioned her over for further comments. "And he's happy to be living here in the United States."

A grower's estate, set in a grove of citrus trees, near Weslaco, Texas, 1948.

Russell Lee

4

ST. MARTINVILLE, LOUISIANA

Race

The picture on page 80 is a mystery today. The place where it was taken, the Purple Circle Social Club on Thirteenth Street in Baton Rouge, Louisiana, in the heart of the black part of town, is now a prosperous brick building rather than a weather-beaten wooden one, but the owner says he doesn't know about anybody who ever held a meeting there. The Louisiana branch of the National Congress of the American People, in the picture the announced sponsor of the meeting, has sunk without a trace. As for the particulars of the meeting, none of the most venerable leaders of the black civic and religious communities of Baton Rouge can remember any kind of organized activity in the spring of 1947 to save the life of Willie Francis. Very few of them even remember who Willie Francis was.

St. Martinville, Louisiana, is a town sixty miles southwest of Baton Rouge, founded in the eighteenth century in the heart of the Cajun country. The supposed trysting place of Evangeline and Gabriel, heroes of

Ely Brown, the caretaker at the Carter Oil Company Refinery in Cut Bank, Montana, 1944.

A worker loading sacks of coffee onto a barge, New Orleans, Louisiana, 1945.

Page 80: Sign on the wall of the Purple Circle Social Club, Baton Rouge, Louisiana, 1947.

Henry Wadsworth Longfellow's syrupy epic *Evangeline*, is under an oak tree on the banks of Bayou Teche just east of the main street of the town. Just before midnight on November 8, 1944, the town druggist, Andrew Thomas, pulled into his garage, got out of his car, and was shot five times in the throat by someone with a .38 pistol. An all-out search for his murderer went on for the better part of a year without bearing fruit. The murder weapon was discovered in a patch of grass, then lost in the mail. On August 5, 1945, police in Port Arthur, Texas, apprehended a black teenage boy who had seen them running after a criminal and had started to run away himself. He had Andrew Thomas's wallet in his pocket. His name was Willie Francis. He was from St. Martinville, one of fourteen children of a subsistence farmer. He had worked part-time in Thomas's drugstore.

In the custody of the Port Arthur police, the boy wrote out the following confession: "I Willie Francis now 14 years old I stole the gun from Mr. Ogise at St. Martinville La and kill Andrew Thomas November 9, 1944 or about the time at St. Martinville La it was a secret about me and him: I took a block pruse will card 128182 in it four dollars in it. I all so took a watch on him and sell it in New Iberia La. That all I'm said I throw gun away 38 pistol. Willie Francis."

He was brought back to St. Martinville and put in jail. He showed the police the spot where the pistol's holster was buried. He was quickly indicted on charges of first-degree murder. He produced a second confession, dated September 12, 1945, which says "Yes Willie Francis confess that he kill Andrew Thomas on November 8, 1944 I went to his house about 11.30 pm i hide backing his garage about a half hour, when he come out the garage I shot him five times. That's all i

remember a short story. Sincerely Willie Francis."

Willie Francis was quickly put on trial in St. Martinville. No transcript was kept, and his lawyers, appointed the morning the trial began, called no witnesses. The jury found him guilty, and he was sentenced to death by electrocution. On the appointed day, May 3, 1946, the electric chair was driven to St. Martinville from the state prison in Angola and set up in the parish courthouse. When they came to get Willie Francis at noon, there was yet another confession scratched into the wall of his jail cell. It read: "I kill Andrew Thomas and today he is lying in a grave and I am not a killer but I wonder where I am going to be lying and in what kind of grave I don't know." Outside the courthouse, a hearse containing a wooden coffin stood by. Willie Francis was strapped in the electric chair, and the switch was thrown. But he didn't die. Some said a weak current had passed through him, some said there had been no electricity at all, but it was plain that the electric chair hadn't accomplished its intended mission.

In 1947, the year Willie Francis would achieve a brief national fame, 81 percent of black families in the United States (about double the white precentage) had family incomes of under $3000, and only one-tenth of a percent had incomes over $10,000 (this was one-thirtieth the white percentage). Segregation of schools and public facilities was perfectly legal and the universal practice in the South—even down to the entrance gates at the huge Standard Oil refinery in Baton Rouge, as you can see from the picture on page 100. Jackie Robinson had just that year broken the color barrier in major league baseball by joining the Brooklyn Dodgers. Of the 849,000 black people in Louisiana in 1940, 147,000 had moved out of the state by 1950. All these

Leonard and Herman Henderson, farm boys in Brown Summit, North Carolina, 1944.

A boy in Abbeville, Louisiana, 1947.

are facts, and they do not begin to tell the emotional truth about Southern race relations then. Unless the population of St. Martinville was extremely unusual, it is certain that every white person waiting outside the courthouse for Willie Francis to die believed that black people were barely members of the same biological species as white people; that some of them felt hate and some did not, but none felt a sense of equality.

But a change was beginning to happen in race relations in Louisiana in 1947—a change of immense and lasting significance, although one that should be considered always in light of the way black people still live, in shacks, on Thirteenth Street in Baton Rouge, and the way the black ghettos of Chicago and Detroit to which all those people moved in the forties look today. The change in race relations is in some ways a cause and in some ways an example of an even larger and more important change, the great force of reform that has emerged since the forties. As reform movements beginning with the New Deal have succeeded, they have created a cumulative assumption that American life should be organized around such abstract ideas as fairness and justice, right and wrong. That in turn has helped to create a national culture in which power resides less in individuals or small communities and more in rules and laws and, almost inevitably, in bureaucracies. These forces are vague when stated so abstractly, but, of course, they touched millions of people at different times and in different ways. In St. Martinville in 1946 they exerted themselves in particular on a young lawyer Bertrand DeBlanc.

On the day after the electric chair failed to kill Willie Francis, Willie's father approached a lawyer he did odd jobs for and asked for his help. The lawyer ap-

Esther Bubley

Children selling berries they have picked, on the road between Houston and Tomball, Texas, 1945.

Eating place on the highway between Houston and Tomball, Texas, 1945.

Esther Bubley

proached Bertrand DeBlanc, who was just back home from the war and starting his practice, about taking on the case. DeBlanc agreed, and began an extremely zealous effort to keep Willie Francis from being put in the chair again. He took the case to the state pardon board three times, the Louisiana Supreme Court three times, and the United States Supreme Court twice, arguing that to electrocute Willie Francis now would violate the Constitution's prohibitions of double jeopardy and cruel and unusual punishment. In addition to the usual legal precedents, DeBlanc invoked the qualities of justice and mercy and the case of Daniel in the lion's den. Even when a firm date was set for the electrocution, DeBlanc was ready to keep appealing, but Willie Francis told him to "leave it alone" because he was ready to die. He was killed in the electric chair on May 9, 1947.

Today DeBlanc lives in Lafayette, Louisiana, fifteen miles from St. Martinville, and practices law with his son Bertrand, Jr., out of a suite of comfortably worn rooms in the back of a house next door to the courthouse. He is a former district attorney, and he keeps his office cluttered with a large collection of books, papers, and memorabilia, in the time-honored manner of country lawyers. I showed him the picture of the sign advertising a mass meeting in Baton Rouge to save Willie Francis, and asked him whether it had been in any sense a civil rights case. Apparently this touched a nerve.

"My approach to the case was, I wasn't trying to stir up controversy," he said. "I just didn't want him to go back to the chair. This was double jeopardy. This was cruel and unusual punishment. The only civil rights was, there was something about did he get a fair trial or something like that. Some groups were interest-

Passengers in the Greyhound Bus Terminal,
New York City, 1947.

Passengers in the Greyhound Bus Terminal,
New York City, 1947.

Todd Webb

Main Street in Monroe, Louisiana, 1947.

A cafe across the street from the Baton Rouge Refinery, Baton Rouge, Louisiana, 1947.

ed in that. But you see, when a person is convicted of a crime, you appeal on a question of law, not fact."

He sketched out the facts of the case for me: "This was a druggist in town. My wife was a clerk in his store. I knew him well. We owned a plot of land together and that's where he got killed. His brother was chief of police. His other brother was head of the police jury. [A police jury is an odd Louisiana institution that is the most powerful body of parish government.] They were an important family.

"He was walking from his garage to his house. Willie was standing there and shot him five times and took the wallet and left. He took the wallet and then he left town. I was convinced he did it. But no man should go to the chair twice. It's not human. From what I can see of the American point of view, people don't like to put a man in the electric chair twice." DeBlanc, small, bright, and voluble, had closed his case.

The only other person still around who had been involved in the Willie Francis affair was Father Maurice Rousseve, a black priest then assigned to St. Martinville, who had twice administered last rites to Willie Francis and twice been in the room when he was strapped in the electric chair. Now he was in Lafayette, at a rectory attached to a small parochial elementary school. He was a small man, but he possessed gravity: he was bald, he peered over his thick black glasses, he spoke in rich, round tones. He said, with deep conviction and in great detail, that Willie Francis had actually been innocent.

Father Rousseve took me into a private room in the rectory to fill me in on his theory. He said Willie Francis had been caught by Andrew Thomas a few days before the murder trying to rob the safe in the drugstore, and

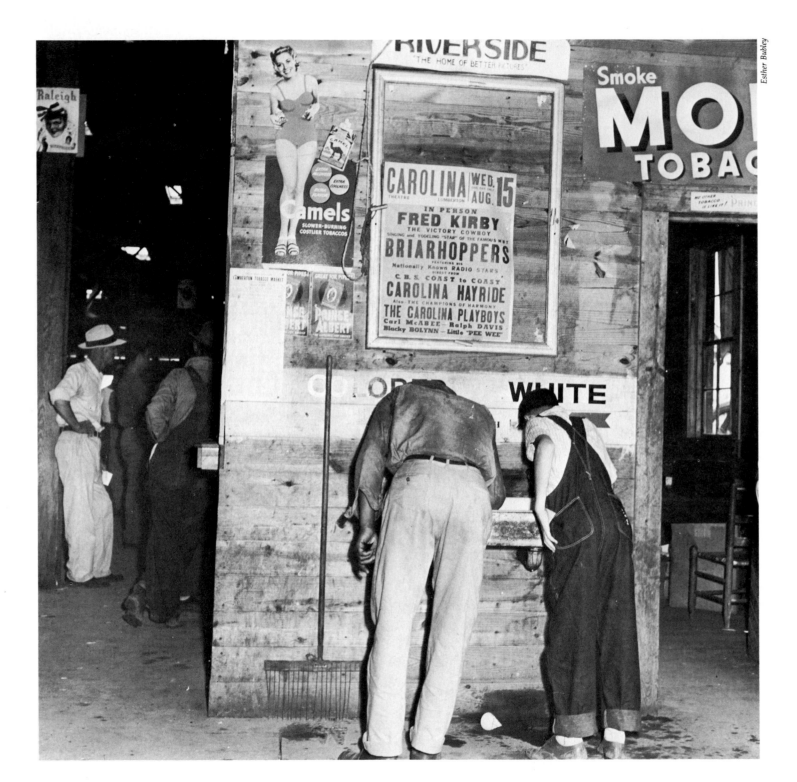

Thomas had kicked him out, thus making the boy someone on whom suspicion might logically fall. But the real motive to kill Thomas lay elsewhere: he was an adulterer, with women black and white, married and single, so there were many men in town who wanted to see him dead. They had had Thomas killed by someone with the precise skill of a marksman, and then convinced Willie Francis, who was simple-minded, to take Thomas's wallet, hide the pistol holster, and confess to the crime, promising they would see to it that he was not punished. This last part of the bargain was fulfilled by the conspirators' grounding the wire from the generator during the first execution, so that no electricity ever passed through the chair. Father Rousseve said he could see that plainly at the time.

He had one suspect particularly in mind, a prosperous farmer named August Fuselier, who he said was a bad man. Once a black man had quit Mr. Fuselier's employ and gone to work for another white man, and Mr. Fuselier, encountering the black man on the road one day, had beaten him. Father Rousseve said Mr. Fuselier was known to have walked into Andrew Thomas's drugstore one night and to have told him to leave his wife alone or he wouldn't live long. The clincher was that Willie mentioned in his first confession that the owner of the murder weapon was "Mr. Ogise," and this to Father Rousseve's mind was a misspelling of "Mr. August," as in August Fuselier, the form of reference being the same black-to-white locution that Willie used when he called DeBlanc "Mr. Bertrand." Anyway, he said, if Willie Francis had done it, why would he carry around the wallet for almost a year? Why had the murder weapon disappeared? Why else would the electric chair have failed? Even Willie Francis's third, jail-cell confession, in the view of Father Rousseve, was part of

Field-workers picking cotton in a field in the Delta country near Belzoni, Mississippi, 1949.

Segregated drinking fountains in a tobacco warehouse, Lumberton, North Carolina, 1946.

the frame-up. Willie was barely literate. White men had written it.

Father Rousseve's outlook on the world was entirely racial. "St. Martinville was always prejudiced," he said. "You know, Southern town. People said, St. Martinville, they used to whip those Negro prisoners at night till you could hear it. There was another case in St. Martinville where there was no justice for the black man. A man had an old mule. And he gave it to a black man. And the mule came up with a colt. Now you know that's extremely rare. And the white man said, 'I never gave it to him.' And he went all around the country showing the mule that came up with a colt, and the black man never got a penny out of it. Oh, yes, Willie Francis. Emmett Till. Viola Liuzzo. Those three workers that were killed in Mississippi. There were a lot of cases in the great civil rights revolution."

On the subject of Bertrand DeBlanc, Father Rousseve's feelings were mixed, but perhaps for that reason they seemed to get to the heart of the matter. On the one hand, for a white man in southern Louisiana to defend a black man in a murder case, and to devote a year's total effort to it besides, was unheard of at the time. It had taken great courage on DeBlanc's part, and he had infuriated the white people of St. Martinville. At the second electrocution, Father Rousseve had overheard one white man saying there should be two electric chairs, one for Willie Francis and one for Bertrand DeBlanc. The lawyer had also been completely honest and sincere throughout.

But Father Rousseve felt, on the other hand, that DeBlanc was a prisoner of the attitudes he had grown up around. "The sad part is this," he said. "He didn't believe the boy was innocent. He would not believe the boy was innocent." Late in the case, DeBlanc had

Sol Libsohn

Clarence Stringfield, a handy man at the Standard Oil terminal in Friendship, North Carolina, 1944.

Men working on the construction of the Brooklyn-Manhattan Tunnel, New York City, 1947.

Louise Rosskam

*A worker in the Flower District,
New York City, 1945.*

turned down entreaties from A. P. Tureaud, a distinguished black lawyer representing the New Orleans chapter of the NAACP, to pursue other aspects of the case, particularly the fairness of Willie's trial. And when it was all over, he had written a letter to the local paper saying he was 100 percent for white supremacy. The case had been DeBlanc's shot at the history books, the product of a young veteran's idealism and ambition; but afterwards, he had moved to Lafayette and settled into a conventional life of local law and politics.

To my mind Father Rousseve's theory of Willie Francis's innocence was too elaborate and left too much unexplained. How could the conspirators have known a year in advance that they would be able to rig the electric chair? Why, if Willie had agreed to confess to the crime, did he decamp for Port Arthur? But there were aspects of his story that did check out. A neighbor had reported seeing a car parked in front of Andrew Thomas's house on the night of the murder, and Willie Francis didn't drive. In the fragmentary official record of the case, there is this unidentified transcript of someone questioning a man named Alvin L. Van Brocklin:

Q: We heard a little rumor that somebody across the bayou might have had something to do with this. Do you know of any associations that he might have had with anybody across the bayou?
A: I saw his car at a lady's house out there several times. . . .
Q: Do you know anything more about the associations of Mr. Thomas and any other woman associates?
A: No sir; that's all I know.

With all the principals in the crime long dead, the actual facts seemed beyond a certain point unprovable;

the side of the case where Father Rousseve's opinions were more plainly right was its racial side. In the first hearing before the parole board, the state's prosecutor had hinted—and of all the details of the case, this one seems the most incredible now—that Willie Francis might be lynched if he were not executed. "We have repeatedly known in the past, unfortunately, of lynchings going on after crimes are committed," he said. "The only way and safest way to keep that from happening is to bring to justice and punish, according to each case, the guilty party." There had also been allegations that the electrocutioners the first time around had gotten drunk in a River Road dive on their way to St. Martinville and purposely kept the power of the electric chair low for the purpose of torturing Willie Francis.

In the month or so before the second and final execution—the period in which the mass meeting at the Purple Circle Social Club in Baton Rouge would have taken place—the momentum in favor of bringing the Willie Francis case into the context of racial relations began to grow. In the earliest records of the case, Tureaud, the NAACP lawyer from New Orleans, is listed as Willie's co-counsel; in records filed closer to the execution, he is not. In the case record there is a curious letter from DeBlanc to the chief deputy clerk of court in St. Martinville, dated May 1, 1947, warning "that some unscrupulous attorney may attempt to initiate some proceedings in this matter," and adding, "I will not hesitate to bring disbarment proceedings against any such attorney." Somebody must have been pressuring DeBlanc to veer away from his strict double-jeopardy defense.

A week later, on May 7, DeBlanc himself changed course slightly by asking the Supreme Court in Washington to reconsider the case based on the drunken-

Gravestone in a black cemetery on Government Street, Baton Rouge, Louisiana, 1947.

Sol Libsohn

A group of foremen confer with a division superintendent about personnel matters in the offices of a Standard Oil subsidiary, Baton Rouge, Louisiana, 1944.

executioner stories. The papers were drawn up by DeBlanc's Washington associate on the case, J. Skelly Wright, later to become a federal judge and a hero of the civil rights movement; perhaps Wright was more eager to pursue that course than DeBlanc was. Wright remembers being called on several months earlier in Washington by a delegation bearing the story of the executioner wanting to torture Willie; DeBlanc told me he never believed that story in the first place. The Supreme Court turned down this final plea, but in a way that made it clear that a new run at the federal court might be in order. That was when the case took its final twist. DeBlanc flew back to Louisiana to talk to Willie Francis, and Willie said to "leave it alone." The decision not to discuss whether the accused had been mistried and mistreated was made, finally, by the accused himself.

The Willie Francis case was the creature of its moment in time. Ten or twenty years later, his murder trial would have been more proper, he would not have been electrocuted in the center of St. Martinville, and if the

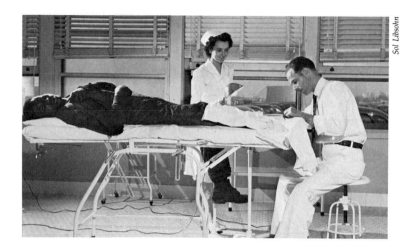

Dr. E. E. Merse and nurse Rose Lafleur suturing the lacerated ankle of Frank Wallace, a worker at the Baton Rouge Refinery, Baton Rouge, Louisiana 1945.

NAACP and other civil rights organizations had wanted to tie the case to larger themes, nobody would have been able to stop them. But ten or twenty years earlier, there would not have been that willingness to stop the local rituals of retribution for a year in order to allow the wheels of the law to spin. The moment of the case was the moment when the old order (tradition, the community, caste) and the new order (rational procedure, national standards, laws) were beginning their final struggle, with Bertrand DeBlanc caught in the middle.

The man in the pictures on pages 102 and 103, the Reverend Julius Rowe, lived in Baton Rouge not far from the Purple Circle Social Club, worked as a porter at the Standard Oil Baton Rouge refinery, and on Sundays conducted services at the New St. Luke's Baptist Church. Too much can be drawn from pictures, but in his case it is clear that in 1947 a black man in Baton Rouge could derive far more dignity from his own community than from the big world of Standard Oil, just as,

Workers leave for home through a segregated plant gate at the Baton Rouge Refinery, Baton Rouge, Louisiana, 1943.

White residential neighborhood near the Baton Rouge Refinery, Baton Rouge, Louisiana, 1948.

oddly, the white people of St. Martinville must have found their tiny corner of the world the easiest arena in which to act out their own views of the stature of the black man. Julius Rowe died in 1973, and his widow, Lena Higginbotham Rowe, 86 years old, lives in a battered white clapboard three-room house in the shadow of an exit ramp from Interstate 10, in the black part of Baton Rouge. Her circumstances offer no obvious signal of progress since the old days.

"He always hold his head up like that," she said when I showed her the picture of her husband in his minister's frock coat. She was a tiny woman, missing many teeth, and sat all gathered up in a bathrobe. "Some folks come down and take that picture from New York. They come and I fixed supper for them. And they played with the baby's cat." Mrs. Rowe went back into her bedroom to get more pictures of her husband. She turned on an ancient window-unit air conditioner that blew feebly and without effect against the summer heat. On the living room wall was a plaque showing the heads of Dr. Martin Luther King, Jr., and his mother set against a background of clouds, over the legend "Together Again."

"He was born in Port Hudson, Louisiana," said Mrs. Rowe, when she had settled into the living room again. "He started working at the Standard when he was fifteen years old for a dollar a day. When me and him married he wasn't making but a dollar a day. When I married him he was a sinner. He got religion in nineteen twenty!"

She leaned forward to make her main point. "He was somebody," she said. She showed me a picture of him at an employees' ceremony at the refinery. "There he is with all the white folks. He was somebody! He was the onliest preacher in town! You see he's

Charles Rotkin

Edwin Rosskam

Julius Rowe at his job, carrying the messages around the grounds of the Baton Rouge Refinery by bicycle, Baton Rouge, Louisiana, 1943.

Julius Rowe at the door of the New St. Luke's Baptist Church with granddaughter Lena, Baton Rouge, Louisiana, 1943.

somebody, don't you?" She looked at me sharply. "*You ain't got that record. I ain't got it. You got to work up to it. He was a man among men. With the white and the colored. Everywhere you look you see him. The Reverend.*" She showed me a picture of her husband in his coffin. "That's his funeral. They took him everywhere in that casket."

Mrs. Rowe walked over to the window, leaned out, and called for her daughter, Lena Mae Chase, the child in the picture on page 103, who lives in a nearly identical house next door with her four children. She graduated from Southern University, a black state school in Baton Rouge where her oldest son had just enrolled as a freshman, and became an elementary school teacher. She said her father was a very religious man, active in civic work. He belonged to the American Legion and the Red Cross. He was especially active, for many years, in the NAACP. He admired Dr. King very much. He had built up New St. Luke's Baptist Church from quarters in an old house to the point where it had a one-room brick building all its own. Looking at his picture again, I couldn't deny that he was somebody, but I wondered if that had been obvious even during those hours when he was consigned to carrying messages through the oil refinery on a bicycle.

I asked Mrs. Rowe and Mrs. Chase whether things had changed much since the forties. "Yes, indeed," said Mrs. Chase. "Things have changed a lot. They're better. I remember the time you had to sit in a certain place on a bus. You couldn't eat at a restaurant. You had to eat standing up and the white folks could sit down. Doctor King changed that."

"We had lamps in the church back then," her mother said. "Now we got electric. We done come a long way."

5

ANDREWS, TEXAS
Leaving the Land

Ever since the first stirrings of the Industrial Revolution, the loosening of people's ties to the land has been the subject of mournful accounts pointing out the organic, simple rightness of the agricultural life and its superiority to the impersonal commercialism of life under industry. In this country, the romance of the rural has been attached not so much to farming (Thomas Jefferson notwithstanding) as to the wilder side of the land—the untamed frontier and its heroic inhabitants, the explorer, the trapper, the scout, and, most of all, the cowboy. The picture on the opposite page has a good deal of that feeling about it. The World War II-era cheesecake poster on the back wall places the picture in the forties, but otherwise the image seems eternal in all its particulars. The cowboy hats and boots, the lariats, the comfortable, weather-beaten clothing, the rough wooden wall in back, the harmonica at the lips of the man in the center, and most of all the solemn and slightly awestruck look on the faces of the boys, which suggests that a way of life is being passed from one generation to another here—all these say that this was a life that was

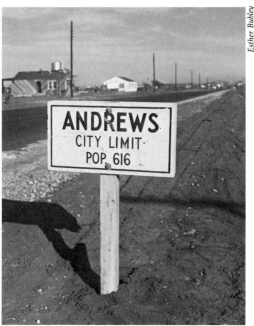

Esther Bubley

Entering Andrews on the town's single paved road, 1945.

A Humble employees' camp in a remote area of South Texas, 1946.

Page 104: Playing cards in the bunkhouse at roundup time, Hayden Miles Ranch, Andrews, 1945.

hard and wild and free and that is no more.

The picture was taken in November 1945 on a ranch just outside the town of Andrews, in far West Texas, a place so remote and possessing so little in the way of nature's bounty that in 1945 its frontier days were still a fresh memory and old-fashioned cowboys had hung on longer than in most places. Change was slow in coming to Andrews because there wasn't much to bring it there. But by the 1940s it had finally arrived, in the form of oil, which lies beneath most of Andrews County. Today there aren't any real cowboys left there; people work as roughnecks or tool pushers instead. The life shown in the picture is gone forever. But it is gone recently enough for it to be possible to find out roughly what its passing really meant: what the exact nature of the old, pre-industrial ties was, and what happened to people when they were loosened. It is still possible to unravel who those cowboys were and what their lives were like.

You get to Andrews by driving thirty-five miles up U.S. Highway 385 from Odessa, Texas, a two-fisted oil-field city set in the middle of the vast Permian Basin fields. The road is ruler-straight; this land was known in the nineteenth century as the Staked Plains because it is so flat and featureless that stakes pounded into the ground by scouts were the only landmarks. Even today, it feels like the end of the earth. The land is unirrigated and untamed: ugly, certainly, but grand because of its endlessness. There are no trees, just grass and scrub. When the land rolls, it takes its time doing so, as if to make even the slightest break in the monotony last as long as possible. The soil is a loose, sandy, light brown; during the three months a year when strong winds are blowing, it whips up into the constant, dispiriting

Harold Corsini

Russell Lee

Cotton bales in the yard of a gin near Vancourt, Texas, 1948.

Corn shocks stacked in a field, Greenbrier County, West Virginia, 1947.

dust storms that have become a staple of local humor (Q: How do you get from Andrews to Odessa in March? A: Open your car doors and sail there.). This was the final part of Texas to be taken away from the Comanche Indians; it wasn't until 1910 that Andrews County was incorporated; it isn't naturally suited for anything but cattle ranching.

Everywhere along the road are pump jacks, the bobbing seesaw-like steel contraptions that bring oil up out of the ground. They bring the eye into the short range when the country demands the opposite and thus work against its peculiar physical appeal. They reinforce the view that industry drains away natural nobility. But when the road gets to Andrews, it becomes instantly clear that nobody there mourns the coming of oil. At the edge of town are signs that read "Welcome to Andrews, Oil Capital of the World" and "Andrews Loves God and Country and Supports Free Enterprise."

John Vachon

In August 1981, when the county celebrated the production of its two-billionth barrel of oil, the lead article in the *Andrews County News* said: "Andrews makes no pretensions: it is an oil town. With all the good and bad things it implies, Andrews was built on oil. Before the oil boom of the early 1940s, Andrews County was just another huge slab of sunburned, semiarid West Texas. It was a poor and sparsely populated region."

In the official county history nearly every family contributed a brief account of itself, and taken together they testify to a way of life back in the ranching days far rougher and bleaker than is commonly ascribed to small towns two generations ago. To quote a few:

"Andrews seemed to be the end of the road."

"The sandstorms were so bad at times we couldn't see the sun for three or four days at a time."

"We used to pray for rain a lot. We used to pray for rain on Sundays in church."

"There were not too many people here and the town sure was not much."

"The struggles to make a living sometimes seemed more than a man could stand, but somehow, somewhere, Bob Moxley seemed to always draw the strength to continue."

"I often say that if I had not firmly believed 'Whither thou goest . . . ' I would have taken my son and gone home to mother."

To the extent that anyone who was not a rancher lived in Andrews County (and the numbers of such people were small; the county's population in 1940 was 600), he had come there only out of the worst conceivable combination of hard luck and false hope. Neill Longley, the boy reading a comic book in the picture on page 110 and the son of the town barber, Dewey Longley, is now a doctor in Houston, and the story he told

John Collier, Jr.

A temporary mess hall built by the government during the war near an oil refinery, Borger, Texas, 1947.

Neill Longley and Carl Lee Underwood in Dewey Longley's barbershop, Andrews, 1945.

Esther Bubley

Jim Parker, an Andrews County rancher who became rich when oil was discovered on his land, 1945.

Mr. and Mrs. Sylvester B. Moore, on their farm near Skowhegan, Maine, 1944.

me about his family's migration to Andrews is typical:

"When I was about four we just couldn't make it anymore in the cafe and barbershop we had in Inadale, so Daddy decided to strike out. We went on the road. We sold pots and pans and Daddy cut hair on weekends. We lived in a tent. If things were good, we'd stay in a town a month. We'd go to San Angelo, Lubbock, Pecos, Fort Stockton. There were hardly any roads. The Model A got stuck a lot. We were in town after town after town, and finally my father came to Andrews. I never could figure out why we settled there. Daddy was a drinking man and Andrews was a dry county, and he spent half his time going to the Moonlight Bar in Odessa."

The ranchers didn't have it much better. In the thirties times were so bad that people were killing their cattle because the government would pay five dollars for a patch of hide. The circumstances in those days of Jim Parker, widely acknowledged as the richest man in the county, are described this way by his daughter-in-law: "In 1933 the loan company again counted the cattle in preparation for taking the mortgaged stock. When they couldn't arrange for their pasture they decided to give Jim $100.00 a month to feed his family and run the three ranches—then both sides prayed for a miracle." Local people say that when oil finally made Parker really rich, as opposed to just Andrews County rich, he couldn't enjoy it because he'd seen too many hard times; look at his picture on this page and you'll see what they mean.

The county's family histories are full of stories of other big ranchers who would wangle jobs delivering the mail or collecting taxes and be off the land like a shot. Even the official Father of Andrews, R. M. Means, a pioneer rancher much beloved for helping to rig the

John Collier, Jr.

1910 election that moved the county seat from the town of Shafter Lake to Andrews, left for Abilene the minute he made a little money. He lived there the last 38 years of his life. The county history says kindly that he "remained a staunch supporter" of Andrews, however.

Oil was discovered in Andrews County in 1929, but the big change can be dated from the moment that Henry Black arrived in town in 1934. Black was the district supervisor in Andrews for the Humble Oil and Refining Company, the biggest domestic subsidiary of Standard Oil of New Jersey, and so without question the most important person in the county. He had been in the oil business since he was fifteen, when he went to work for Texaco as a roughneck, and had worked his way up. In 1926 he brought in the Yates oil field near Iraan, Texas, for Humble. Eight years later he drilled the discovery well in the Means field, on the ranch of the Father of Andrews. As was the company's custom when it established a major new operation in a remote area, Humble built, under Black's direction, a company camp. It was eight miles north of the town of Andrews, had trees and a recreation hall, and was eventually home to 52 families. The camp made Henry Black sole ruler of a village nearly the size of Andrews, as well as the personification in the county of the biggest oil company in Texas and dispenser of by far the richest patronage available. He was not known as a sweet or gentle man, but he was respected. To be hired by Henry Black meant you could get married and raise family. That was where the cowboys came in: they all wanted to work for Humble.

In 1941 Andrews County's second oil field, the Fullerton, was discovered, and in 1947 it was joined by the Dollarhide and Shafter Lake fields. Andrews be-

Gordon Parks

A contestant in the pulling competition, with his team of oxen, at the Windsor County Fair, Maine, 1944.

A milk cow being put up for auction on a ranch in the Wind River Valley of Wyoming, 1947.

Russell Lee

A traveling crew of wheat harvesters eating breakfast before dawn,
near Vernon, Texas, 1949.

came a boom town. There was over-crowding, brawling, a housing shortage, and an unseemly pregnancy or two. Almost every week somebody died in the heavy nocturnal traffic of people headed to the county line to get a drink; one of these was Carl Lee Underwood, Jr., the lonely-looking boy standing next to Neill Longley and gazing at the cowboy boot in the picture on page 110. Nobody complained much about the upheaval, given what had gone before. In the fifties Andrews settled down and became a prosperous town, with an excellent school system and a powerful football team. Its fortunes varied with the world oil market—down in the sixties, up in the seventies with the OPEC price increases, and most recently down with the oil glut—but never in a way that remotely recalled the old days. Today the town's population is 11,000. There are four or five places to eat, and paved roads, and because of the schools, people are confident that their kids will be able to go on to college and do well in life. Everybody knows that the reason things got better was the oil.

Part of N. R. Hamm's traveling wheat
harvesting operation, near Vernon, Texas, 1949.

Children in a temporary government housing project, Andrews, 1945.

G. N. Timmons and two of his thirteen children, Jimmy and Melvin, in the tent where they lived on the outskirts of Andrews, 1945.

The gaunt and desperately poor man in the picture on page 119 is G. N. Timmons, and with him are two of his thirteen children, Jimmy and Melvin. The picture was taken in 1945 in the old Army tent on the edge of Andrews where the Timmonses lived, without lights or running water, sleeping three to a bed. G. N. Timmons is long dead now, but Jimmy and Melvin still live in Andrews. I went to see them at Jimmy's house, which he built himself, a couple of miles outside of town. It is a one-story white house made of concrete blocks, carpeted and wood-paneled and comfortably furnished inside. Next door on the same lot is a small mobile home where their mother lives.

Jimmy is a lean, jug-eared, redheaded man, and he obviously didn't find it pleasant to look at the photograph. "I wouldn't want a picture like that flashed around," he said. "Those was hard and hungry times."

Melvin disagreed. "I'm not ashamed," he said. "That's the way it was for a long time for us. Hell, we went two and three days without food. It was really rough. We were worse than the people in the ghetto. I wouldn't never go back to that. No way. That's what keeps me going."

"I'll tell you one thing," said Jimmy. "Before I'd let my kids go through that, I'd steal. I'd *never* go through it again."

They told me some of their family's history. They were by birth and tradition farm laborers. They pulled and hoed and chopped cotton for a living. They would work a harvest, buy a dilapidated car with the proceeds, and drive on to the next harvest. In 1939 the Timmonses worked the harvest in Gatesville, Texas, bought a '29 Chevy, and headed west in search of a big cotton crop in northern Mexico that they'd heard about, they got as far as El Paso and ran out of money and gasoline.

Esther Bubley

Landscape near McCamey, Texas, 1945.

Somebody stole a bunch of bananas so they could eat, and somebody else traded his pocketknife for gasoline, and finally they made it to the cotton fields. They pulled cotton for a couple of weeks and saved ten or fifteen dollars, but then the work ran out and they had to go on the road again. They headed north, for the cotton fields near Lubbock. But in Andrews they ran out of money again, so Andrews became their home.

I asked Jimmy how he and Melvin escaped a life of poverty. "The oil field," he said without hesitation. "All of us went to the oil fields just as soon as we could. That's all there was to it. And the oil field's been great to us. We're not rich, but we live a good medium life."

Why hadn't their father gone into the oil field, then? "He tried it," Jimmy said. "He roustabouted once

A clerk at a Baton Rouge refinery makes out a delayed birth certificate for an employee who has no records except his family Bible, Baton Rouge, Louisiana, 1945.

for a while. But he always wanted to go back to farming. Farming's all Daddy ever knew. That's what he grew up around. He didn't like any part of the oil field. He thought it was . . . just oily, that's all."

Today seven of the thirteen Timmons kids work in the oil business. Jimmy and Melvin both went into well servicing, and both worked their way up from the floor to tool pusher, a supervisory position that pays about $30,000 a year and is about as high as you can go in the business without any education. Then they quit their jobs to start their own well-service company. Their good fortune pales next to that of the ranchers in Andrews County, all of whom are rich from oil royalties now, but that doesn't mean it should be dismissed. A life around machines extracts its price—like many peo-

Esther Bubley

ple in the oil field, Jimmy Timmons is missing part of a finger—but it is a sure route out of desperate poverty. For those who were not quite so poor, leaving the land paid off in a slightly more subtle way: it meant freedom from living utterly under the control of someone else.

The picture of the cowboys playing cards in the bunkhouse, on page 104, was taken on the Hayden Miles ranch just to the west of the town of Andrews. Miles was in a business partnership—the Black and Miles Cattle Company—with Henry Black, the Humble superintendent. Black leased some land near the Humble camp, and they ran the cattle back and forth. Out of the arrangement Miles got the use of Black's land, and in addition it was well known that anybody connected with the Humble company had easy access to pipe, fence, and other invaluable equipment. Black got instant membership in the community of ranchers in the county, from whom oil leases had to be bought, and ranching allowed him to assume the role of the traditional figure of respect in West Texas.

In the picture, the man sitting on the floor in the foreground is Mack Dunn, an old-timer who cowboyed up and down the West, never staying in one place for long. The man watching and playing the harmonica is Ruel Lowe, who was Hayden Miles's ranch foreman for many years. The boy on the left and the boy in the middle, looking at Ruel Lowe, are W. H. and Dan Black, Henry Black's boys. The young man on the right, in the flat hat, is one of the Craddock boys, sons of a large family of small ranchers. It might be Will Ed or Thomas Joe or Billy D.; nobody knows for sure.

In 1946, the year after the picture was taken, Henry Black left Humble and, in partnership with a rich man from the nearby city of Midland, Texas, started the

Russell Lee

Wheat being piled in a warehouse, Altus, Oklahoma, 1949.

Moving cattle through a dipping vat to rid them of lice, Hayden Miles Ranch, Andrews, 1945.

Henry Black Drilling Company. He moved to Midland and got rich himself. He owned seventeen drilling rigs and a company plane and a large spread in Brazoria County, on the Texas Gulf Coast, where he grew up. W. H. and Dan learned how to cowboy as kids, but there was never the slightest chance they'd actually become cowboys. They were going to become oilmen. When they finished college, they went into their father's business and eventually took it over from him.

When oil exploration went sour in the late fifties, the two brothers sold off the company's drilling rigs. Even before that, a seven-year drought forced their father to sell most of his cattle in Andrews County. They bought more land in Brazoria County and trucked what was left of their cattle there. Now Dan lives in Midland, invests in oil drilling projects and looks after some real estate investments. W. H. lives in Richmond in Brazoria County and runs the ranch, while at the same time selling off slices of it for development into new suburbs of Houston. Both of them have wonderful memories of the old days in Andrews before oil got to be so big. They told me about the cowboys they had known, about cold December mornings on the ranch, about missing school for roundup, about getting up before dawn and riding to faraway grazing lands, about sleeping out and eating chuckwagon food. They said people were friendlier then and there was more space and money didn't matter much. They talked about Hayden Miles, the gruff, crusty old rancher who had helped build Andrews County.

Of the real cowboys in the picture, Mack Dunn didn't leave much of an impression on people in Andrews. He must have moved somewhere else after a short time. But the story of the other cowboy, Ruel

Lois Westfall, the wife of the foreman on a sheep ranch in West Texas, feeds Jean Spilsbury, her granddaughter, 1945.

Willie and Gene Bishop, newlywed hands on a West Texas sheep ranch, eating dinner, 1945.

125

Esther Bubley

Dan Black mounting a horse on the Hayden Miles Ranch, Andrews, 1945.

Henry, W. H., and Dan Black, with Ruel Lowe (his face partly observed, on the right), in a card game in the bunkhouse of the Hayden Miles ranch during roundup, Andrews, 1945.

Lowe, the ranch foreman, was well known to everyone in town. Hayden Miles had taken Ruel's wife Irma as his mistress, and she lived with him in the main house, while Ruel lived next door in the bunkhouse with the other cowboys. As people in Andrews remember it, Hayden Miles was not so much tough as mean. His wife and daughters lived in Midland, where the girls' school was, and he was the absolute ruler of his spread in Andrews. The cowboys who worked for him liked cowboying, but one by one they drifted into the oil field because Hayden Miles paid so poorly. Those who, like Ruel Lowe, couldn't bring themselves to leave cowboying didn't have any choice but to work for Miles. People remember that Ruel once made up his mind to get work at another ranch, but Miles gave him a raise and he stayed. Miles could control people and force them to put up with the deepest indignities, in the pre-oil days in Andrews.

Hayden Miles had one son, Jay, who was going to inherit the ranch, but when World War II came along Jay enlisted, to his father's dismay, and he was killed in action in 1943. When Miles died, in 1958, the ranch was run by the bank until two local men, Gene Irwin and Max Ramsey, bought it from his estate. Ruel Lowe moved into town and got a reputation as a drinking man. He died in 1962. Irma Lowe married the sheriff in another town in West Texas and still lives there today.

I wondered how Hayden Miles had felt about Ruel Lowe: Fond, or guilty? It seems clear that Ruel would have been better off in the oil field than on the Miles ranch as far as money and independence went, but perhaps there was some sort of bond between the two men, something deeper than the rational economics of the oil field could ever provide.

On an impulse, I went down to the courthouse and

Esther Bubley

*Eating at a chuck wagon during roundup,
Hayden Miles Ranch, Andrews, 1945.*

*Gene Tomberlin, who checks on an oil pipeline
on horseback, waves to a friend,
West Texas, 1945.*

looked up Hayden Miles's will. He died on April 30, 1958, and left a gross estate valued at $344,499, of which he bequeathed half to his wife and half to his daughters. But he put in a special clause, which reads like this:

"I further direct that my executors and trustees shall pay to RUEL LOWE for so long as he lives, the same salary which he is receiving at the time of my death . . ." Maybe he decided to make it up to Ruel in the end. ". . . provided, however, that such payment shall cease at any time he terminates his employment with my estate." Then again, maybe what he really wanted, even dead, was to maintain authority over the cowboy's life.

Ruel Lowe's successor as foreman of the old Hayden Miles ranch is Bill Price, a wiry, friendly, weather-beaten man of 56 who has worked on the ranch all his life, as did his father and grandfather before him. Price lives in a white converted mobile home on the ranch with his wife. In the living room, where he spends his free time, there is wall-to-wall shag carpeting, a color television set, and plush imitation brocade furniture. Price has a few cattle of his own on the ranch, in addition to the owners' cattle. The oil field eventually drove up the price of even ranch labor, and he is the beneficiary of that.

Next door to the mobile home is the bunkhouse of the picture, where Ruel Lowe lived. It is built of red brick, and is tiny as a shack. A couple of recent arrivals from Mexico live there now. Over on the other side of the mobile home is where the ranch house used to be, where Hayden Miles lived. It burned down one night in 1968. Bill Price's brother died in the fire. The homesite is ringed by pump jacks; otherwise you can't see anything from it but open country.

6

TOMBALL, TEXAS
The New World

The group in the picture on the opposite page, tranquilly domestic, is the Tanner family—Jimmie, Velma, and Gene, the youngest of their three sons (you can see the older sons if you look closely; they're the sailors, then off at war, whose pictures are hanging over Jimmie's left shoulder). On page 133 is a picture of the Tanners saying grace before dinner. On page 132 they're relaxing in their backyard. On page 134 Gene is playing with his dog. There are a couple of points to notice especially in these pictures: in the backyard picture the unpainted wood of the house; in the living room picture, the bare light bulb hanging over the dinner table. Given that the pictures aim to show how good the life lived by plain people in the employ of the Humble Oil and Refining Company was, they are now a testament to how perceptions of an appropriate level of household comfort have risen in a generation.

The Tanners then lived—Jimmie and Velma still live—in Tomball, Texas, a small town thirty miles northwest of Houston that was then completely dominated by Humble Oil. When the Tomball oil field was discov-

Esther Bubley

ered in 1933, Humble approached the town with a proposition: if it could have the mineral rights to the whole town, the townspeople could have free gas forever, courtesy of Humble. Tomball accepted. It was a sleepy town with the feel of the South and not much intrinsic cause for prosperity, and it has always been eager to become a company town for whatever company would have it. In 1906 the railroad came through and the townspeople were so grateful that they named their community (previously known as Peck) after the railroad's lawyer, Thomas H. Ball of Houston. When the Humble Company arrived, it treated the town to a program of determined paternalism the likes of which will surely never be seen in this country again. The schools were good. The streets were clean. The mayor was a Humble employee. Just north of town, Humble built two employee camps, one for its supervisors and one for its blue-collar workers (who built their own houses from materials supplied by Humble), and these housed 300 families, more than lived in town. They were called the upper camp and the lower camp by the company, but everybody called the lower camp "poor boy camp." That was where the Tanners lived.

Roy Stryker sent Esther Bubley to Tomball in the spring of 1945 for three months, the longest any of the Standard Oil photographers spent in a single place. She produced a detailed record of nearly every aspect of the life of the town: school and church, work and leisure, family life and social life. Her pictures were received at the time as proof of the goodness of small-town life—*Coronet* magazine printed some of them under the title "Oiltown, USA"—and indeed, that's the way most of the people in the pictures remember those days. There was an order to life, and a comfort that came from not wondering whether things were as they should be.

The Tanner family saying grace before dinner, Tomball, 1945.

The Tanners in their backyard, Tomball, 1945.

Page 130: The Tanner family—Velma, Jimmie, and their son Gene—at home in the Humble "poor boy" camp, Tomball, 1945.

133

Esther Bubley

Gene Tanner and his dog, Sergeant, Tomball, 1945.

George Nicklow, Humble Oil's district supervisor in Tomball, in his living room in the Humble upper camp, 1945.

Some of Bubley's pictures of the town, with horse-and-buggies in the main street and ladies in homespun dresses, bring to mind the nineteenth century; to be in a modern industrial setting in itself represented for most of the townspeople a vast leap in luxury and convenience past what they had known a generation earlier. What seems by today's standards an astonishing degree of civic regularity seems to have come naturally then. Everybody went to church, and, at the proper moment in life, most of them were duly baptized. The women played cards in their "study club," the men dominoes. Boys joined the Boy Scouts and went out for football and off to war. The height of public raciness was the town pool hall. By and large people liked the Humble Company and accepted its primacy in their lives.

"Nice town, very nice," says George Nicklow, who as Humble superintendent ran the town and whose picture is on page 135. He lived in a long succession of god-forsaken oil boom towns before coming to Tomball —Smackover, Arkansas; Breckenridge, Texas; Healdton, Oklahoma; Harp, Texas—and later tried Houston. Tomball is where he retired on his Exxon pension and long-accumulated stock. His daughter married a member of Tomball's most prominent family, the Kleins. He is well pleased with Tomball. "Quiet town, nice folks. We used to work seven days a week here with one week's vacation. Seventy-five cents an hour, five dollars a day, and no overtime. Exxon was good to us. They was like a father to us. Lord, they made a millionaire out of me."

By the early 1960s the Tomball field was pretty well played out. The Humble camps were gone, their day having passed in both the most immediate and the most general sense. You can still see the Humble houses scat-

Esther Bubley

Roy Ford eating lunch in the elementary school, Tomball, 1945.

The Nicholson family at home in the Humble camp, Tomball, 1945.

tered around town, bought by Tomball families and hauled away from the camps. The end of the oil boom didn't cause the town to wither away, because by that time Houston was becoming a big city and people in Tomball could commute to jobs there. Conversely, as Houston grew, it sent waves of economic activity northward that by the seventies had reached Tomball. Today Tomball is an extremely prosperous town, and the reason is its proximity to Houston. There is a brand new Safeway, a McDonald's, and a thirty-six-acre commercial development is underway. The countryside around the town is dotted with signs out in the fields, announcing the coming of one or another subdivision with an English name: Kensington, Clarendon. It would seem comic that anyone could dream of making money by imposing British Victorian imagery on the piney farmlands of near East Texas, except that it will surely work.

The children of the Humble camps have done well in this new world. Roy Ford, the boy in the picture on this page, sold his family's automobile dealership in 1979, just before the bottom dropped out of the auto business, and retired on the proceeds. Of the three Nicholson children, shown with their mother on page 137, Danny has the Century 21 real estate agency in Tomball, Barbara just opened a personnel agency in Houston, and Ben Wayne owns a trucking company. Gene Tanner, Jimmie and Velma's son, has been especially successful: the only one of the Tanner boys to go to college, he graduated from the University of Houston, went to work for a cement company poetically named Ideal Basic Industries, and rose to the position of vice president for sales in the Southwestern region, with a large private office in a new building near the Houston airport.

Today Jimmie and Velma Tanner, well into their eighties, live in a green house on an acre and a half of land on the outskirts of Tomball. When I went to see them, Velma, who is sick, said very little, but Jimmie talked a blue streak. It became apparent that he had gotten to like being perceived as a character, and slipped easily into that role; it was also apparent that to understand exactly what kind of character he was required keeping in mind that he was born in the last century, and that he had a quick mind that was substantially free of formal education. At Humble he was a pumper, charged with going around to completed and producing oil wells and regulating the flow of oil, a job he performed for many years on horseback.

He greeted me wearing a belt with a big, enameled buckle in the form of the old Humble logo, and without needing any prodding he began to talk.

"I came here to Tomball the twenty-sixth day of December, nineteen thirty-three," he said. "I was born in Vicksburg, Mississippi, the twenty-first day of July eighteen ninety-six. I'm a Rotarian. I joined the Humble Company in June of nineteen nineteen.

"My daddy was a brick mason. We left Vicksburg when I was twelve and moved to Houston to find work. My daddy had a cousin who was a brick mason there. When I was thirteen I went to work myself. I took a job as an elevator operator in a two-story building. Then I graduated to office boy. I moved around. I ran a filling station in Houston. I met my wife at a dance at Beech's auditorium on Main Street in Houston. I started with Humble in Baytown, Texas. I was in the rigging department. Then Goose Creek, Texas. Then Evergreen, Texas. I left Humble three times, I don't remember why. But I could always go back because my boss said I was a good hand. But he said don't quit no more. I retired

Two students at Tomball High School at a ceremony honoring one of their schoolmates who was killed in the war, 1945.

First grade students at the Tomball elementary school pledging allegiance to the flag, 1945.

Hardy Gilliam, the manager of Klein's Checkerboard feed store in Tomball, on the front porch of the store, 1945.

in nineteen sixty-one with thirty-five years.

"Now, we lived in the Humble camp. We lived down in poor boy camp—that's where the fellas who done all the work lived. The white-collar guys lived in another camp." I asked him if this had bothered him. "Was I mad? Oh, no. We could raise a garden where we were. They even furnished our pipe. The Humble Company was really good for us. I got a granddaughter today that's fourteen years with Humble." (It is the practice among former Humble employees to fail to use the company's new name, Exxon.) "She's a computer analyst."

He moved on to broader themes. He showed me a letter President Carter sent him on his sixtieth wedding anniversary. He told me about the time he saw John Philip Sousa lead a band. He said he spells his name Jimmie because any old boy can call himself Jimmy. Then he rummaged in a desk drawer and pulled out his poetry, written for delivery at family occasions, and, especially, at Rotary Club functions. The sheet he gave me made no sense, but Jimmie explained that this was because he wrote down only the first line of each poem, and once he saw the first line he could remember the rest. The first few first lines went like this:

> *I try to live a good*
> *I was born in Mississippi*
> *You may travel the whole*
> *I had lots of sweethearts*
> *We lost a little grandson*
> *Dangerous sum the Jew*
> *Take time to smell*
> *Let your handshake*
> *I married my wife*

A street in downtown Houston, 30 miles from Tomball, 1945.

Esther Bubley

I read a few out loud and Jimmie provided the rest. For example, the full version of "I married my wife" was:

> *I married my wife in 'twenty-one*
> *And believe you me it's the*
> *Best thing I ever done.*

One of the poems he had written out in full:

> *You may travel this world over*
> *From Maine to Tennessee*
> *And have friends in all these places*
> *From towns to sea to sea*
> *But when I come home to Tomball*
> *My heart is filled with glee*
> *For my friends in Tomball Rotary Club*
> *Are the dearest friends to me.*

Of the other first lines, the ones that most piqued my curiosity were the ones I didn't dare ask him to render in full, so I let the matter rest. Jimmie showed me to the door. "I say this," he said, by way of parting advice. "The Lord designed the world one time. If these kids today don't brace up, he's gonna do it again." He fixed me with a big grin. "Nicholas," he said, heartily, "gimme five." We shook hands and he clapped me on the back. "That's my Rotarian greeting. Hospitality! Hospitality! Come back and see us!"

From Tomball I drove directly to see Gene Tanner, Jimmie's son, who lives only twenty minutes or so away from Tomball, toward Houston. Gene lives off of a highway that circles Houston twenty miles from downtown, called Farm-to-Market Road 1960. FM 1960 is completely within the orbit of the city, a long and bus-

In the pool hall, Tomball, 1945.

Four oilfield hands in front of the City Cafe after dinner, Tomball, 1945.

143

Diane Witlin

Workers completing construction of Shoppers' World, a new suburban shopping center in Framingham, Massachusetts, 1951.

Cecil Faris, the mayor of Tomball and owner of a Humble gas station, announces the Allied victory in Europe, Main Street, Tomball, 1945.

tling suburban commercial strip. Although nothing there is more than ten years old, already the real estate ads refer to "the tradition and prestige of the FM 1960 area," and this is especially true of the section of 1960 where Gene lives, which is known, with a nod toward the residents' view of themselves, as Champions.

Although FM 1960 is jammed with small shopping centers punctuated with large malls, you'd have to look hard to find a church there, or a cafe, or a pool hall, or even people standing around. The old forms are not present. It seemed to be a community devoted, in a very safe way, to human pleasure. Gene had remarked to me earlier that the Humble poor boy camp of his youth might have been a better place to raise kids than the Champions area. There was less community here, less discipline, and, frankly, people just weren't as hungry.

Esther Bubley

Mildred McGowan, Noreen Cannon, F. K. Rose, and C. H. Shaw singing during evening services at the First Baptist Church, Tomball, 1945.

A new cloverleaf intersection in the New Jersey suburbs just west of the George Washington Bridge, 1949.

Gene lives in a large brick house in a subdivision named Huntwick, which is populated mostly by people who work in Houston but were born and raised somewhere else—Michigan, North Carolina, Misssouri, all over. When I got there the Tanner family was gathered around the station wagon, preparing to go out to Gene's ranch for the weekend. In Texas owning a ranch is still an important indicator of success, and Gene says that the ranch reminds him of his boyhood and is, he feels, probably good for the kids, too. He was dressed cowboy-style, in boots, blue jeans, and a western-cut shirt, which connoted ties to the land, although people in the Tomball of the forties certainly didn't dress that way. Whereas Jimmie Tanner, who had knocked around a lot in his life and didn't have much money, seemed to have plenty of free time, Gene, who had been with the same company since college, risen steadily, and made enough money to be able to spend impressively on the accoutrements of leisure, was in a hurry. We trooped through the living room—big, with a high, beamed ceiling—and into the kitchen, where I spread out the pictures. The kids were restless, ready to get in the car.

Gene picked out the picture on page 130 and pushed it across the table to his son Richard, who was wearing a T-shirt that said, "and on the eighth day God created YAMAHA!" I wondered if his grandfather would consider it blasphemous. A wonderful yellow light was streaming into the kitchen through the windows, causing all the appliances and fixtures to shine.

"Look, Richard," said Gene, flushed with sentiment. "I was just about the same age you are right there in that picture."

"So what?" said Richard, and he ran outside to the station wagon.

About the Author

Nicholas Lemann is executive editor of *Texas Monthly*. He has also been an editor of the *Washington Monthly*, and a reporter for the *Washington Post*. His first book, *The Fast Track*, was published in 1981, and his magazine journalism has appeared in many national publications, including *Harper's*, *The Atlantic*, *New York*, *The New York Times Book Review*, and *The New Republic*.

Lemann, born and raised in New Orleans, now lives in Austin, Texas.